Classical Guitar Favorites

Alfred Music Publishing Co., Inc.

Los Angeles

International Standard Book Number: 978-0-7390-6875-5

Printed in the United States of America

Published under agreement by Alfred Music Publishing Co., Inc.

Distributed by Alfred Music Publishing Co., Inc. and Penguin Group (USA) Inc. All rights reserved.

Contributing Editor: *Thomas Kikta*

Cover Photo: *Classical guitar by Robert Ruck.*

Interior Photos: *Photography by Tim Kikta; Matt Kikta, model*

Recordings: *All CD selections recorded at*
Brookside Studios, Upper St. Clair, PA
Thomas Kikta, guitar

Contents

Reviewing the Basics

Getting to Know Your Classical Guitar 1

The Parts of the Classical Guitar 1

Playing Positions 2

Using Your Right Hand 3

Sounding the Strings 5

Basic Organization of Right-Hand Finger Movement 7

Using Your Left Hand 10

Tuning Your Guitar 12

The Basics of Music Notation 14

Reading Guitar Tablature (TAB) 19

Approaching Interpretation and Expression 20

Pieces

Moorish Dance (Aaron Shearer) 22

Country Dance (Ferdinand Carulli) 24

Andantino (Mauro Giuliani) 26

Españoleta (Gaspar Sanz) 29

Menuett in A Minor (Johann Philipp Krieger) 32

Menuett in D Major (Robert de Visée) 34

Exercise No. 18, Op. 35 (Fernando Sor) 37

Exercise No. 17, Op. 35 (Fernando Sor) 41

Exercise No. 22, Op. 35 (Fernando Sor) 44

Minuet in G Major (Johann Sebastian Bach) 49

Minuet in G Minor (Johann Sebastian Bach) 53

Etude in E Minor (Dionisio Aguado) 56

Saltarello (Anonymous)..62

Spanish Romance (Romanza) (Anonymous)..........................67

Lágrima (Francisco Tárrega)...70

Prelude (Francisco Tárrega) 72

Etude No. 3, Op. 60, in A Major (Matteo Carcassi).................74

Etude No. 7, Op. 60, in A Minor (Matteo Carcassi) 79

Pavane No. 1 (Luys Milán)...84

El Noi de la Mare (Catalan Folk Song) 89

Greensleeves (Anonymous Elizabethan Folk Song) 92

Leyenda (Isaac Albéniz) 96

Jesu, Joy of Man's Desiring (Johann Sebastian Bach)..............105

Bourrée in E Minor (Johann Sebastian Bach).....................109

Variations on a Theme by Handel (Mauro Giuliani) 112

Canon in D (Johann Pachelbel) 116

Guardame las Vacas (Luis de Narváez)...........................121

Classical Gas (Mason Williams) 125

Ashoken Farewell (Jay Ungar)......................................130

Simple Gifts (Elder Joseph Brackett).............................134

Appendixes

Appendix A: Music Theory 1-2-3..........................141

Appendix B: Guitar Fingerboard Chart...............151

Appendix C: Suggested Reading, Listening,
and Guitar Organizations 153

Appendix D: Music History Timeline...................155

Appendix E: Common Italian Music Terms 159

Appendix F: Glossary 163

Introduction

Like many guitarists, you have found fingerstyle to be a big part of why you enjoy the guitar. Taylor, Jorma, Mayer, and Buckingham all have a special place in your playing, and now you want to take it a step further into the realm of classical guitar to experience Bach, Giuliani, Tarrega, and Segovia. No doubt, the intimate details of holding the classical guitar, approaching it with your hands, using your fingers to play it, and, ultimately making a beautiful tone, can be a rather involved affair. Don't let that stop you! This book is an "in a nut shell" introduction to fundamental ideas that assists you in applying them to some of the most popular pieces in the repertoire. This collection, along with suggested method books and a teacher, is a very entertaining and effective way to explore the world of classical guitar.

We all play the guitar for pretty much the same reason—to play our favorite pieces. It's so easy to get caught up in mastering the technical issues, learning to read music, and understanding music theory that we can spend hours at the instrument and still not have a good selection to play. Note-reading, technique, and theory are all good tools—but that's all they are. This is your chance to put all those tools together to play beautiful music.

Learning your favorite pieces and discovering new ones is the most important musical experience you have. All the selections in this book use related chords, scales, techniques, and other elements, so as you learn your favorite selection, you will also learn the skills you need to play other favorites as well.

Fundamental information is provided at the beginning of the book to help you play every selection. First, there is a review of the basics, like holding the classical guitar, sounding the strings, and reading music and TAB. Then, each selection is introduced with a short presentation exploring the details that make it easier to play. Important concepts students tend to overlook are outlined here and brought to your attention so that a greater level of success might be achieved. Historical perspectives are also explored, and "behind the scenes" trivia gives life to the performers, composers, and their works. All the music is shown in standard music notation as well as TAB to assist you in approaching the score.

The enclosed CDs provide recordings of all the selections in this book. In addition to hearing your favorites, you may discover new selections that will inspire you to play. Listen to them often, and keep them handy as you learn each song. See more about the special features of the CDs on the following page.

Remember that it's not important to master every aspect of every piece. You can focus on the parts that grab your attention the most—the melody, an interesting section, or anything you want to play. As you gain experience, technique, and knowledge, putting the pieces together and learning the complete selections will become easier and easier.

Be sure to check out the other books in this series to see if there are other favorites you'd like to learn. If you want more information about playing the guitar, reading music, or even writing your own music, there are lots of other Complete Idiot's Guides to help you along.

Now tune your guitar, dig in, and most importantly—HAVE FUN!

How to Use This Book

Some people approach learning an instrument by isolating all the technical skills, and through years of study and practice, they develop a command of those skills. Others simply learn by having a friend show them a simple selection and then proceed to learn on a piece-by-piece basis. Some combination of the two methods is probably the best, but you should always spend a good portion of your music time learning selections that you would really love to share and perform for your friends and family—or just for yourself.

Every selection in this book is presented in standard music notation and tablature (TAB). Reading music is a skill acquired through diligent practice, and it has many benefits. For fretted instruments, the use of tablature predates music notation and offers a quick way of knowing what to play without having to be an accomplished music reader. Providing TAB to show exactly where to fret each note in conjunction with standard music notation can be an ideal way to get you up and playing right away. All the detailed information, such as rhythm, fingerings, and expression, is found in the standard music notation.

Start by picking a selection you really want to play. If this is your first experience with the classical guitar, stick to the first six or so selections in the book. If you're not sure, listen to the CD and decide which selection you might want to play. Music is an aural art, so always have the sound of the piece clearly in your head before you attempt to learn to play it on the guitar.

Next, before attempting to play your chosen selection, read through the lesson that precedes it, and practice any suggestions. The selections are easiest at the beginning and progress to more difficult levels. Basic concepts are introduced with the first pieces, and additional techniques are introduced as needed when required for specific selections. Each lesson is broken into various sections, with handy sidebars along the way to point out things that are particularly important, interesting, or helpful. New and useful terms are italicized and defined either in the lesson itself or in the glossary at the back of the book. You may find it best to use this book in conjunction with other books listed in Appendix C, and it can be a fine supplemental source of repertoire to help you apply the concepts you learn from your method book or with your teacher. The performances provided on CD are a point of reference for hearing phrasing, expression, and simply to hear how the piece goes. With these tools, you are provided with the fundamental concepts needed to approach each of these pieces successfully and gain further insight as to how to apply your developing technique.

The disc and track number of the piece on the included CDs. The TNT software allows access to play-along, looping, and tempo options. See the TNT instructions on the next page.

A brief introduction to the piece.

The main body of the lesson, with tips, pointers, excerpts, examples, and other helpful information.

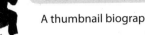

GUITAR GODS

A thumbnail biography of an artist or composer.

DEFINITION

Definitions of key terms used in the text.

TIP

Additional help, insight, and advice on topics in the lesson.

FUN FACT

Interesting trivia about the artist or the piece.

If you want to know more about music theory, be sure to read Appendix A: Music Theory 1–2–3. It will teach you about scales, the circle of fifths, intervals, chords, and how they relate to each other.

Appendix B is a diagram of the guitar fretboard, showing every note on every string up to the 12th fret.

Appendix C is a list of suggested reading and listening. Here you will find suggested classical guitar methods as well as books on the history and background of the classical guitar. You will also find a list of classical guitar recording artists, provided for your listening pleasure, and some guitar organizations to check out.

Appendix D is a music history timeline that puts the lifetimes of performers and composers in context with other great musicians and world events occurring at the same time.

Appendix E contains a list of common Italian terms used in music notation, such as tempo markings and directions for expression.

Appendix F is a glossary that covers all the terms used in the book.

About the TNT Tone 'n' Tempo Changer Software on the CD

The TNT software on the CDs can be accessed using a computer and allows you to change the tempo of the recording, faster or slower, to suit your ability and preference. For complete instructions, see the TnT ReadMe.pdf file on the disc.

Windows users: insert a CD into your computer, double-click on My Computer, right-click on your CD drive icon, and select Explore to locate the file.

Mac users: insert a CD into your computer and double-click on the CD icon on your desktop to locate the file.

Trademarks

All terms mentioned in this book that are known to be or are suspected of being trademarks or service marks have been appropriately capitalized. Alfred Music Publishing Co., Inc. cannot attest to the accuracy of this information. Use of a term in this book should not be regarded as affecting the validity of any trademark or service mark.

Acknowledgements

All text, arrangements, and fingerings are by Thomas Kikta. CD selections performed by Thomas Kikta on a 1987 Thomas Humphrey Millennium guitar and recorded at Brookside Studios, Upper St. Clair, PA.

The author would like to thank Aaron Stang and Kate Westin for all their priceless help and guidance on this project, Matt Kikta and Tim Kikta for photography, and Matt Kikta for being a guitar model.

A special thank you to my best friend and lovely wife, Patti, for without you none of this would be possible.

About the Author

Thomas Kikta is the Director of Classic Guitar at Duquesne University, where he has held the position since 1987. Having worked with Aaron Shearer for almost 30 years, Mr. Kikta is a leading authority on his teachings and co-authored the third edition of Shearer's best-selling method *Classic Guitar Technique*, Vol. 1, which was nominated for Best Instructional Book or Video for 2009 by Music and Sound Retailer. Kikta is a co-founder and vice president of the Aaron Shearer Foundation, an organization dedicated to preserving and propagating the teachings and legacy of the revolutionary guitar pedagogue. As co-founder and board chairman of the Guitar Society of Fine Arts, Mr. Kikta has brought a decade of world-class guitar music to Pittsburgh audiences as well as free music lessons for underprivileged children. He resides in Pittsburgh with his wife and four children. To ask questions or discuss details of this book, visit Mr. Kikta at www.thomaskikta.com.

Reviewing the Basics

Getting to Know Your Classical Guitar

You may or may not be able to name all the parts of your guitar, and you may not need to. If you ever get into a conversation with another guitarist, however, it will probably go better if you know what is being referred to as "the head nut" or "the bridge nut."

The Parts of the Classical Guitar

Note that there are two customary methods of securing a string to the bridge, as seen here. We recommend method No. 1 for all six strings. Important: The turn of the string completing the knot must be behind the back edge of the bridge.

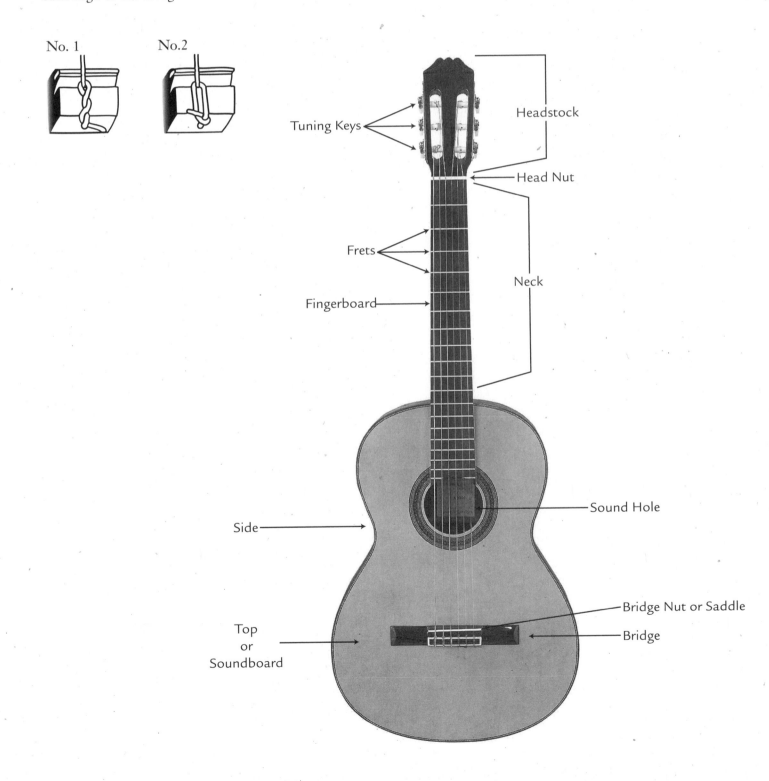

No. 1   No.2

Tuning Keys

Headstock

Head Nut

Frets

Neck

Fingerboard

Sound Hole

Side

Top
or
Soundboard

Bridge Nut or Saddle

Bridge

Playing Positions

The most important aspect of positioning the classical guitar in relation to your body is having complete access to the entire range of the fingerboard and strings without sacrificing muscular alignment in your shoulders or back.

The traditional means of supporting the guitar while playing is the foot stool.

Other methods of holding the guitar developed over time. The A-frame does a good job of keeping the instrument in the area that allows access to the entire fingerboard without misaligning the back.

Sitting with foot stool.

The Shearer Strap holds the guitar in proper position while sitting or standing.

Sitting with Shearer Strap.

Standing with Shearer Strap.

The right method for maintaining a good seated position is a personal choice that requires some experimentation. Be open minded, and remember that as your repertoire becomes more difficult you must refine your position to accommodate the demands of the piece.

Note: If you find yourself leaning towards the fingerboard, the instrument is too low and should be raised up and moved towards the right. (See p. 10.) And always remember there should be no pain associated with playing the guitar!

Using Your Right Hand

The classical guitarist uses the fingers and thumb to sound the strings rather than a pick. This allows the player to create *polyphony*, meaning music with multiple voices; instead of simply strumming chords or picking single notes, the classical guitarist can play a melody, harmony, and bass line all at once. The majority of today's classical guitarists use their fingernails to help produce a beautiful, round, projecting sound. Other schools of thought throughout history, however, believe that a warmer sound is produced by using just the flesh at the tip of the finger and no fingernail. In the beginning, you will probably start with no nails on your right hand, since it will take some time to grow them out. This will give you time to experiment with tone production, and you will quickly learn that this experimentation with tone never ends.

The Right-Hand Fingers

When playing classical guitar, the thumb generally plays the bass notes, which generally will be notated with the note stems pointing down. The fingers play the melody and inner harmony voices, which will be notated with the stems pointing up. The fingers are labeled using Latin abbreviations, as illustrated here.

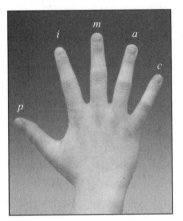

p = pollex

i = index

m = medius

a = annularis

c = cuatro

Labels of the right-hand fingers.

Approaching the Strings

The right hand should approach the guitar as shown in the following photographs. Notice that the wrist is straight when viewed from the top and gently arched when viewed from the side. The fingers are positioned midway between total *flexion* and *extension*, also know as the *midrange position*.

Top view.

Side view.

Do not allow your hands to look like the following pictures in any way!

Hand is arched too high.

Hand is arched too low.

Wrist is deviating downward, causing the hand to deviate upward.

Wrist is deviating upward, causing the hand to deviate downward.

As you begin to sound the strings, make sure you contact the strings with your fingertips rather than allowing your fingers to go down into the strings so that the finger pads make contact. If you have fingernails, the string should rest between the nail and flesh; notice that the thumb also contacts between the nail and flesh, with both touching upon preparation. If you do not have nails, make your contact point with the string as close to the end of your finger as possible. Be sure that your tip joints are firm and do not collapse.

Contact the string with the fingertip, between the nail and flesh.

Sounding the Strings

The classical guitarist uses two different types of strokes to play the guitar: *rest stroke* and *free stroke*.

Rest Stroke and Free Stroke

Rest stroke produces a louder, warmer sound and is used for scale passages or to accentuate any melodic line. By itself, the rest stroke is a *monophonic* stroke, allowing only one string to ring at a time; once the finger sounds a string, it rests against the adjacent string. Beautifully harmonized chords are not possible with the rest stroke.

Classical guitarists primarily use free stroke, since it allows multiple strings to ring together and create chords and intervals. After a finger sounds a string, it passes *freely* over the adjacent string, thus allowing all strings involved to ring *freely*. Free stroke is what you see fingerstyle guitar players use, whether they're performing classical, country, pop, rock, new age, or any other music that requires multiple strings to ring simultaneously.

Since free stroke is used primarily in this book, we'll focus on it to get you up to speed so you can start enjoying the music selections.

Placing the Hand

Place your hand on the strings as shown in the photo. Notice that the hand is placed in its midrange position, thus allowing for maximum leverage.

This is the foundational position, with which all activity begins.

Sounding a String with the Thumb

Place your hand as shown in the photo, with the thumb prepared on the 5th string and the fingers prepared on the 3rd, 2nd, and 1st strings.

Preparation for playing with the thumb.

To sound the string, flex your thumb from the *wrist joint* (the joint where it meets the wrist). Avoid the tendency to move the thumb at the tip joint or middle joint. After sounding the string, allow the thumb to follow through until it bumps into the side of the *i* tip joint, as seen here.

Yes, the goal is to sound the strings, but it is important to allow the finger to *follow through* without impeding its motion. This will create a good transfer of energy from the thumb to the string and allow the thumb to go through its natural cycle of flexion and extension.

After playing, the thumb follows through until it meets the tip joint of the index finger.

Sounding Strings with the Fingers

First, place your hand as shown in the photo.

Hand placement for playing with the fingers.

Sound the top three strings simultaneously with fingers *i*, *m*, and *a* using free stroke, passing freely over adjacent stings to allow them to ring freely. This simultaneous motion of the fingers is called *sympathetic motion*. Make sure your pinky (*c*) is moving along, too. Don't ever let it stick out. This basic movement between thumb and fingers is used to play chords with alternating bass notes, or four-voiced chords in which the thumb and fingers all play simultaneously.

Fingers moving in sympathetic motion.

It's very important to maintain proper right-hand position when playing. As you prepare the pieces in this book, get in the habit of checking that your right-hand position doesn't tend to wander. The two most common errors are made in the position of the wrist and the follow-through of the fingers. The arch of your right wrist is important to maintain, as shown on page 3. If the wrist is collapsed, there is no room to follow through with your fingers; if the wrist is too high, you'll feel strain since you have no mechanical advantage. Keep the wrist midway between its total flexion and extension. The other issue is to follow through with your fingers after you have sounded the string. Do not make an effort to stop the finger, but allow it to pass beyond the point that it sounded the string and follow through toward the palm. This allows the right transfer of energy from the finger to the string and enables the muscles in your fingers to go through their natural timing of flexion and extension.

Basic Organization of Right-Hand Finger Movement

A simple way of looking at right-hand organization is that the right-hand fingers are either *alternating* or *moving sympathetically*.

Alternation

Here's an example of *alternation*: While finger *i* sounds the string and follows through, *m* extends to prepare to sound the string. Then, as *m* sounds the string and follows through, *i* extends. As one finger is in, the other is out, and vice versa, as shown in the following figures showing alternation between *i* and *m*.

Preparing to sound the string with i.

As i follows through, m extends.

As m follows through, i extends.

As i follows through, m extends.

The alternating motion technique is used to play scales and single-note melodic lines like the one below. When alternating, be sure not to repeat a finger in succession. For example, *i–i* or *m–m* will make this line sound very choppy. Be sure to alternate *i–m–i–m*, just like walking left–right–left–right. Practicing on scales such as this will begin to reinforce the habit of alternating.

Once you feel comfortable with *i* and *m* alternation, practice the above exercise with *m* and *a* alternation. Be sure to have *i* move along with *m*, and *c* move along with *a*. Do not hold any finger still, because doing so will cause tension. While *m* and *a* are playing, *i* and *c* should move along with them. This will give you valuable practice using the *a* finger. Do not let your pinky stick out!

Sympathetic Motion

Sympathetic motion is used to play chords or multiple voices simultaneously. The fingers move together to sound two or three strings at once or as an *arpeggio*.

Fingers preparing to sound a three-voice chord using sympathetic motion.

Fingers after moving sympathetically to sound the chord.

Fingers playing an arpeggio with sympathetic motion, sounding i, then m, and then a.

Fingernails

As your nails begin to grow in, you should maintain a smooth, round nail that is free from any rough edges.

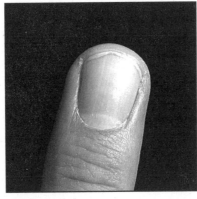

Proper nail shape.

As the *i*, *m*, and *a* nails grow out, you can begin to create a plane on each nail as shown here, using a sapphire-type nail file. The string will travel on this plane when sounded.

The *p* nail is also shaped with a plane, but the angle of the file is very low in relation to the plane of the nail. This way, the thumbnail can work in a down-stroke very similar to a *plectrum* or pick on a steel-string guitar.

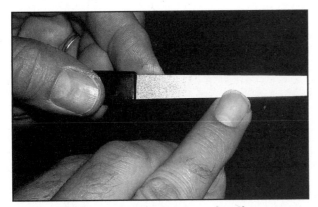

Using a nail file to create a plane on each nail.

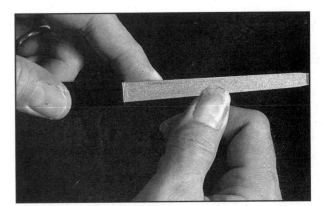

Shaping the plane of the thumbnail.

About the Right-Hand Fingerings Used in This Book

Right-hand fingerings are written above the music staff with thumb markings below the staff. To keep from becoming too monotonous, right-hand fingerings are indicated only where they change; continuous or repeating patterns are indicated once, and new fingerings are only indicated when a change is necessary or a tricky section comes along. For instance, if you see *i* and *m* alternating, you can assume it is going to continue that way until new fingerings are indicated. Also, remember that a note with a down-stem will usually be played by *p*. Be sure to look carefully at the notation, as using the proper right-hand fingerings is critical to the ease and success of playing the piece. Don't be afraid to pencil in any fingerings that you feel you need—it's a good habit that really helps. A given passage can often be fingered different ways, and it will still work. In those cases, do what feels most comfortable to you. You can expect more difficult right-hand techniques to be introduced as they are needed for various selections as you play through the book.

Using Your Left Hand

As previously mentioned in the section about positioning the guitar, it is important that you position the instrument so that your left hand has access to the full range of the fingerboard without leaning your torso to the left or dropping your left shoulder to access notes. The following photos demonstrate these incorrect positions.

Avoid leaning your torso to the left.

Do not drop your left shoulder to reach notes.

The left hand should approach the fingerboard so that the thumb stays on the neck while the hand maintains a midrange position.

Left hand in midrange position.

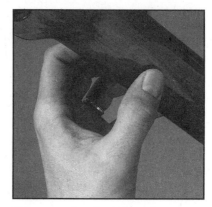

Keep your thumb on the neck.

Do not allow your thumb to stick up above the neck as seen here.

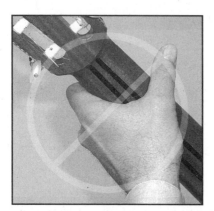

The thumb is too high.

When stopping a string, be sure that your finger is placed directly behind the fret to get the cleanest possible sound.

Stop the string directly behind the fret to produce a clear tone.

The Left-Hand Fingers

The fingers of the left hand are numbered as shown here.

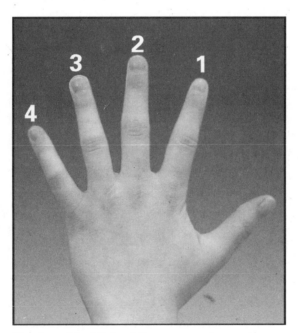

Numbers of the left-hand finger.

About the Left-Hand Fingerings Used in This Book

The beginning selections in this book generally stay in an area of the neck called the *open position*. The open position covers the open strings as well as the first four frets of the instrument. With open position fingering, any note on the 1st fret is held by the 1st finger, any note on the 2nd fret is held by the 2nd finger, and so on. If a series of notes deviate from open position fingering, then the fingers to use will be indicated with numbers next to the notes.

It's important to realize that numbers alone indicate fingers, while numbers inside circles ① ② indicate strings. Also, to reduce clutter and make the music easier to read, fingerings are not indicated on repeated passages, but you should get in the habit of penciling them in when needed. New, more complex left-hand fingering concepts will be explained as they are needed for various selections throughout the book.

Tuning Your Guitar

Every musician knows the agony of hearing an instrument that is not in tune. Always be sure to tune your guitar every time you play, and softly check the tuning every now and then between selections.

About the Tuning Pegs

First, make sure your strings are wound properly around the tuning pegs. They should go over the top of the peg as shown in the illustration. Turning a tuning peg clockwise makes the pitch lower, and turning a tuning peg counter-clockwise makes the pitch higher. Be sure not to tune the strings too high, or you run the risk of breaking them. Also, be sure to keep your classical guitar tuned to a reference pitch of 440 Hz. Classical guitars do not have a truss rod in the neck, and anything higher than an A-440 reference will put undo stress on the instrument.

TIP

Always remember that the thinnest, highest-sounding string, the one closest to the floor, is the *1st* string. The thickest, lowest-sounding string, the one closest to the ceiling, is the *6th* string. When guitarists say "the top string," they are referring to the highest-sounding string, and "the bottom string" is the lowest-sounding string.

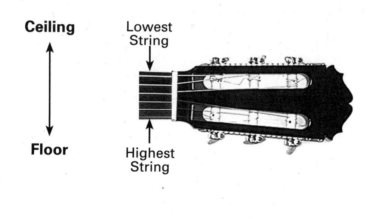

Tuning Using the Included CDs

If you pop one of the included discs into your CD player, you'll notice that the first track is a tuning track. For your convenience, both CDs have the tuning track.

The first note plucked is the 1st string, and the track continues through the 2nd, 3rd, 4th strings, and so on. So one by one, make sure the pitches of the strings on your guitar match the notes you hear on the tuning track. Just adjust your tuning pegs accordingly. It may be difficult at first, but with practice and lots of attentive listening, it'll come naturally.

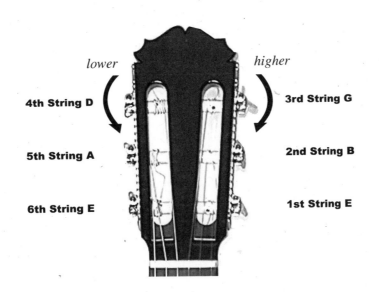

lower   higher

4th String D   3rd String G

5th String A   2nd String B

6th String E   1st String E

Tuning the Guitar to Itself

The day will surely come when your guitar is out of tune but you don't have your trusty play-along CDs with tuning tracks. If your 6th string is in tune, you can tune the rest of the strings using the guitar by itself. The easiest way to tune the guitar is with an electronic chromatic tuner. A chromatic tuner can also be used for *altered tunings*. There are many types available, and a salesperson at your local music store can help you decide which is best for you and show you how to use it.

The 6th string is tuned to E below middle C.

If you have access to a piano, tune the 6th string to the note E below middle C.

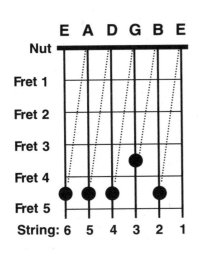

To tune the rest of the strings, follow this sequence:

- Press 5th fret of 6th string to get pitch of 5th string (A).
- Press 5th fret of 5th string to get pitch of 4th string (D).
- Press 5th fret of 4th string to get pitch of 3rd string (G).
- Press 4th fret of 3rd string to get pitch of 2nd string (B).
- Press 5th fret of 2nd string to get pitch of 1st string (E).

The Basics of Music Notation

Standard music notation contains a plethora of musical information. If you don't already read notation, you will probably benefit from studying the following fundamental concepts. Understanding even a little about reading notation can help you create a performance that is true to the original.

Notes

Notes are used to indicate musical sounds. Some notes are held long and others are short.

Note Values		
whole note	𝅝	4 beats
half note	𝅗𝅥	2 beats
quarter note	𝅘𝅥	1 beat
eighth note	𝅘𝅥𝅮	½ beat
sixteenth note	𝅘𝅥𝅯	¼ beat

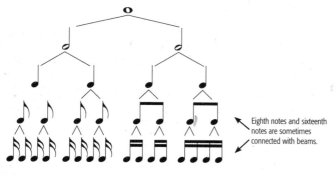

Eighth notes and sixteenth notes are sometimes connected with beams.

Relative note values.

When a *dot* follows a note, the length of the note is longer by one half of the note's original length.

Dotted Note Values		
dotted half note	𝅗𝅥.	3 beats
dotted quarter note	𝅘𝅥.	1 ½ beats
dotted eighth note	𝅘𝅥𝅮.	¾ beat

A *triplet* is a group of three notes played in the time of two. Triplets are identified by a small numeral "3" over the note group.

Quarter-note triplet.

Rests

Rests are used to indicate musical silence.

Rest Values		
whole rest	▬	4 beats
half rest	▬	2 beats
quarter rest	𝄽	1 beat
eighth rest	𝄾	½ beat
sixteenth rest	𝄿	¼ beat

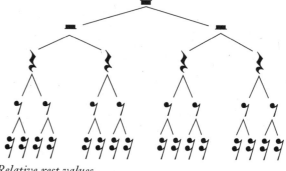

Relative rest values.

The Staff

Music is written on a *staff* made up of five lines and four spaces, numbered from the bottom up. Each line and space is designated as a different pitch.

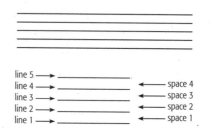

line 5 ⟶ _____
line 4 ⟶ _____ ⟵ space 4
line 3 ⟶ _____ ⟵ space 3
line 2 ⟶ _____ ⟵ space 2
line 1 ⟶ _____ ⟵ space 1

The staff is divided into equal units of time called *measures* or *bars*.

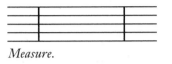

Measure.

A *bar line* indicates where one measure ends and another begins.

Bar line.

A *double bar line*, made of one thin line and one thick line, shows the end of a piece of music.

Double bar line.

Notes on the Staff

Notes are named using the first seven letters of the alphabet (A B C D E F G). The higher a note is on the staff, the higher its pitch.

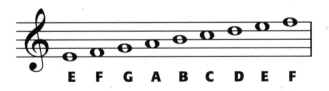

E F G A B C D E F

The *treble clef*, also called the *G clef*, is the curly symbol you see at the beginning of each staff. The treble clef designates the second line of the staff as the note G.

Here are the notes on the lines of the treble staff. An easy way to remember them is with the phrase "Every Good Boy Does Fine."

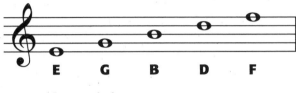

E   G   B   D   F

Notes on the lines.

Here are the notes on the spaces. They are easy to remember because they spell the word FACE.

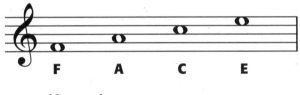

F   A   C   E

Notes on the spaces.

The staff can be extended to include even higher or lower notes by using *ledger lines*. You can think of ledger lines as small pieces of additional staff lines and spaces. The lowest note in the following figure is the open low E string of the guitar.

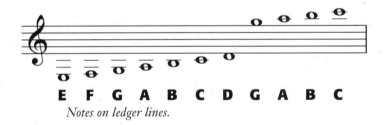

E F G A B C D G A B C

Notes on ledger lines.

Accidentals

An *accidental* raises or lowers the sound of a note. A *sharp* ♯ raises a note one *half step*, which is the distance from one fret to another. A *flat* ♭ lowers a note one half step. A *natural* ♮ cancels a sharp or a flat. An accidental remains in effect until the end of the measure, so if the same note has to be played flat or sharp again, only the first one will have the accidental. See the Guitar Fingerboard Chart in Appendix B for all the flat and sharp notes on the guitar up to the 12th fret.

HALF STEPS • NO FRET BETWEEN

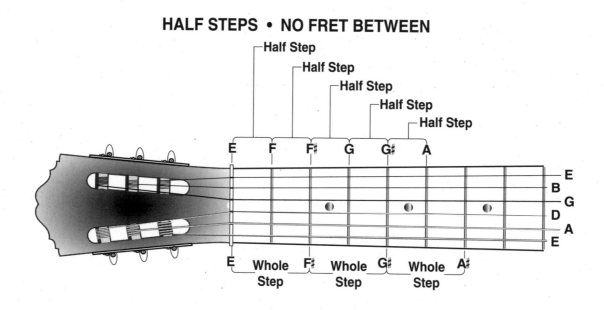

WHOLE STEPS • ONE FRET BETWEEN

Key Signatures

Sometimes certain notes need to be played sharp or flat throughout an entire piece. In this case, it's easier to put the sharps or flats in the *key signature* instead of putting an accidental on each individual note. If you see sharps or flats at the beginning of a staff just after the treble clef, that means to play those notes sharp or flat throughout the music. The key signature can change within a song as well, so be sure to keep an eye out. Below are two examples of key signatures.

Play each F, C, and G as F♯, C♯, and G♯.

Play each B and E as B♭ and E♭.

Time Signatures

The *time signature* is a symbol resembling a fraction that appears at the beginning of the music. The top number tells you how many beats are in each measure, and the bottom number tells you what kind of note gets one beat. Most pieces of music have the same number of beats in every measure, but the time signature can also change within a piece. It's important to notice each time signature and count correctly, otherwise you could end up getting ahead or falling behind.

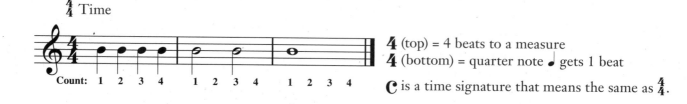

$\frac{4}{4}$ Time

Count: 1 2 3 4   1 2 3 4   1 2 3 4

4 (top) = 4 beats to a measure
4 (bottom) = quarter note ♩ gets 1 beat

𝐂 is a time signature that means the same as $\frac{4}{4}$.

3 = 3 beats to a measure
4 = quarter note ♩ gets 1 beat

6 = 6 beats to a measure
8 = eighth note ♪ gets 1 beat

9 = 9 beats to a measure
8 = eighth note ♪ gets 1 beat

12 = 12 beats to a measure
8 = eighth note ♪ gets 1 beat

TIP

A whole rest always means rest for a whole measure. So in ¾ the rest is three beats, in ⁶⁄₈ it is six beats, and so on.

Ties

A *tie* is a curved line that joins two or more notes of the same pitch, which tells you to play them as one continuous note. Instead of playing the second note, continue to hold for the combined note value. Ties make it possible to write notes that last longer than one measure, or notes with unusual values.

Hold B for five beats.

The Fermata

A *fermata* 𝄐 over a note means to pause, holding for about twice as long as usual.

Pause on notes with a fermata.

Repeat Signs

Most pieces of music don't start and then ramble on in one continuous stream of thought to the end. They are constructed with sections that are repeated in some organized pattern. To avoid having to go through pages and pages of duplicate music, several different types of *repeat signs* are used to show what to play over again. Repeat signs act as a kind of roadmap, telling you when to go back and where to go next, navigating you through the piece.

Repeat Dots

The simplest repeat sign is simply two dots on the inside of a double bar. It means to go back to the beginning and play the music over again.

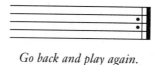

Go back and play again.

When just a section of music is to be repeated, an opposite repeat sign at the beginning of the section tells you to repeat everything in between.

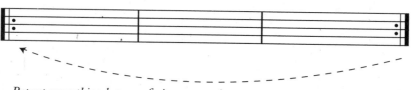

Repeat everything between facing repeat signs.

1st and 2nd Endings

When a section is repeated but the ending needs to be different, the *1st ending* shows what to play the first time, and the *2nd ending* shows what to play the second time. Play the 1st ending, repeat, then skip the 1st ending and play the 2nd ending.

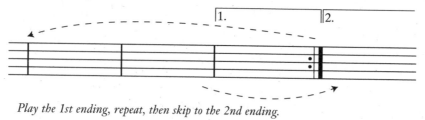

Play the 1st ending, repeat, then skip to the 2nd ending.

Other Repeat Signs

D.C. al Fine	Repeat from the beginning and end at **Fine**.
D.C. al Coda	Repeat from the beginning and play to the coda sign ⊕, then skip to the **Coda** and play to the end.
D.S. al Fine	Repeat from the sign 𝄋 and end at **Fine**.
D.S. al Coda	Repeat from the sign 𝄋 and play to the coda sign ⊕, then skip to the **Coda** and play to the end.

Reading Guitar Tablature (TAB)

Tablature, or *TAB* for short, is a graphic representation of the guitar fingerboard. By indicating a string and a fret, the TAB provides the grid location of any note. Although standard notation gives you all the information you need to know to play a piece, including detailed information about rhythm, fingerings, slurs, ornamentation, and expression, the TAB staff tells you quickly where to finger each note on the guitar. The bottom line of the TAB staff represents the 6th string, and the top line is the 1st string. Notes and chords are indicated by the placement of fret numbers on each string.

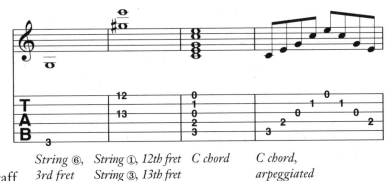

String ⑥,   String ①, 12th fret   C chord   C chord,
3rd fret   String ③, 13th fret   arpeggiated

The following are examples of various guitar techniques you might come across in the notation of the songs. Unless otherwise indicated, the left hand does the work for these.

Articulations

Hammer-on: Play the lower note, then "hammer" your left-hand finger onto the string to sound the higher note. Only the first note is plucked.

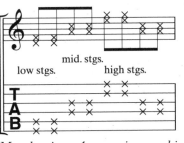

Muted strings: A percussive sound is produced by striking the strings with the right hand while laying the fret hand across them.

Pull-off: Play the higher note with your first finger already in position on the lower note. Pull your finger off the first note with a strong downward motion that plucks the string, sounding the lower note.

Palm mute/pizzicato: The notes are muted (muffled) by placing the palm of the right hand lightly on the strings, just in front of the bridge.

Legato slide: Play the first note, and with continued pressure applied to the string, slide up to the second note. The diagonal line shows that it is a slide and not a hammer-on or a pull-off.

Harmonics

Natural harmonic: Lightly touch the string with the fret hand at the note indicated in the TAB and pluck the string, producing a bell-like sound called a harmonic.

Artificial harmonic: Fret the note at the TAB number, then use a right-hand finger to lightly touch the string 12 frets higher than the fretted note, and pluck the string with an available right-hand finger or your thumb.

Approaching Interpretation and Expression

Self expression is one of the primary reasons for playing a particular piece of music; to take a selection that you find appealing, then put your personal touch to it and make it your own is a powerful motivation. If everyone approached a piece of music the same way or played it exactly as written, matters would be quite boring indeed and one would lose interest pretty quickly. One must realize that the music notation is nothing more than a snapshot of the composer's intentions, and therefore it is only a starting point as every artist interprets the piece a little differently. While a rock musician gets to blaze searing leads, and a jazz musician, after playing the head, improvises lines based on the original melody, the classical musician is given specific notes, rhythm and harmonies, and the only latitude for improvising is by adding interpretation and expression.

The tools the musician uses to achieve this include dynamic variation (soft or loud), rhythmic note grouping (rubato), color variation, touch (legato or staccato), and tempo. The amount of variation and degree of contrast are totally up to the musician and will vary from performance to performance based on the artist's emotion, historical understanding, and taste.

After reading this you are probably asking, "Well yeah, but how do I get started?" The best approach is to listen to other musicians—not just those playing the piece you are learning, but playing music in general. The recordings that accompany this book are a starting point. You should also listen to performances by other artists. Many times you will borrow ideas from various sources and mold an interpretation into your own. It is the same way you learned to communicate with speech, by listening to how others group words and change inflection and dynamics to get ideas across.

You will begin to understand what a logical grouping of notes sounds like and what stylistic considerations are called for based on when a piece was written. For example, a selection from the romantic period, like "Lagrima," might employ far more rubato than a baroque selection like "Bourrée."

A lot goes into interpretation, and the process will never end. For the rest of your life you will be refining your ability to "shape a line." So don't be afraid—give it a try! First learn a selection slowly with proper fingerings, notes, and rhythm. Remember tempo markings are targets, so work slowly until you feel comfortable. Be patient and avoid confusion and error. As you're doing this, think of ideas you might want to try. As you become comfortable with the piece, try to experiment and incorporate these expressive ideas into the work. Don't be timid—I would rather a student overdo it a bit than do nothing at all. The degree of variation can always be dialed back.

Realize this takes time. Perhaps weeks or months might pass before you truly feel comfortable to fully express a piece the way you want. Have fun with it, and enjoy using your imagination and creative side to make a selection a personal art form all your own.

Pieces

Moorish Dance
Aaron Shearer (1919–2008)

Key Thoughts

The first six selections in this book were chosen for their fun and interesting melodies, and also because they reinforce some basic classical guitar techniques that are essential for success. With that, it's fitting we apply your basic knowledge of classical guitar technique with this simple piece written by Aaron Shearer, whom many consider to be the father of American classical guitar. Shearer wrote "Moorish Dance" in 1959 for his historic instructional series *Classic Guitar Technique*, and it is the perfect simple piece to apply basic thumb movement while moving *i* and *m* together in sympathetic motion.

Take Note

When playing "Moorish Dance," it's important to follow through after sounding the string. This is similar to the follow-through necessary when striking a golf ball or baseball, as it allows full transfer of energy from the nail to the string and permits the muscles to go through their natural timing of flexion and extension. When the thumb sounds and follows through, the fingers extend to play again, and while the fingers sound and follow through, the thumb extends to play again. The follow-through and this alternation between thumb and fingers are the foundation of this exercise.

TIP

At first, practice playing just the notes for the thumb. This will give you a chance to apply the thumb motion introduced in the section "Using Your Right Hand." It's perfectly fine to anchor or rest your fingers on the treble strings while doing this. Once you feel comfortable, try anchoring the thumb and just playing the notes for *i* and *m*. Again, this will help you apply the motion necessary for playing with the fingers. When a level of comfort is reached with these separate movements, combine them to play the piece as written.

GUITAR GODS

Cited by the Guitar Foundation of America as the most prominent classical guitar teacher of the 20th century, **AARON SHEARER** trained many of today's greatest performers. After starting the first collegiate classic guitar program at American University, he went on to head programs at Catholic University, Peabody Conservatory, and the North Carolina School of the Arts. He taught last at Duquesne University. Shearer's efforts produced such great artists as Manuel Barrouco, David Starobin, David Tannenbaum, and Ricardo Cobo. Although he passed away in 2008, his work is carried on by the Aaron Shearer Foundation, which you can visit at www.aaronshearerfoundation.org.

Moorish Dance

Aaron Shearer

Country Dance
Ferdinand Carulli (1770–1841)

Key Thoughts

"Country Dance," by Ferdinand Carulli, is from the *classical period*, which occurred roughly from 1750 to 1820. Like the previous piece, this selection reinforces the sympathetic movement of *i* and *m*, but it also introduces alternation of *i* and *m* on single lines. Later, in the third section, an arpeggio using *p–i–m–a* in sympathetic motion is introduced.

Take Note

When doing alternation in the right hand, you want to start with a finger that will not cause a *cross fingering*. A cross fingering occurs when a finger that normally plays a higher string crosses to play a lower string. An example of this can be seen in measure 21 where *i* is sounding the 3rd string and *m* is sounding the 2nd string; starting the measure with *m* would create a cross fingering because *m*, the higher finger, would play the lower string while *i* would have to try to play a higher string. Sometimes a cross fingering cannot be avoided in more complex material, but we want to generally minimize them as much as possible. In simple material, cross fingerings can almost always be avoided. The right-hand fingerings in "Country Dance" do not allow any cross fingerings.

TIP

When you play the *p–i–m–a* arpeggio, be sure that all the fingers flex together and extend and reset together when *p* plays. It's a good idea to isolate those two measures in the third section (measures 17 and 18) until you are comfortable with this new technique. (See page 57 for a complete explanation of the *p–i–m–a* arpeggio.)

GUITAR GODS

FERDINAND CARULLI was born in Naples, Italy, and was recognized as a famous virtuoso guitarist, composer, and musical author. Although he received his first musical training on the cello and didn't discover the guitar until he was 20 years old, he is credited with writing the first complete guitar method in 1810, titled *Harmony Applied to the Guitar, Op.27*. After moving to Paris, where he spent the rest of his life, he wrote 400 guitar pieces in the span of 12 years—that's an average of nearly three selections a month!

Country Dance

Allegretto ♩ = 100

Ferdinand Carulli

Andantino
Mauro Giuliani (1781–1829)

Key Thoughts

If there was a "high priest" of Vienna's 1808 guitar cult movement, it was Mauro Giuliani. A composer, virtuoso performer, and teacher, Giuliani elevated the guitar from an instrument used mostly to accompany voice or violin to a full-fledged solo powerhouse. Though simple, this "Andantino" sets the stage for the important concept of *polyphony*, creating the illusion of two guitars by using *i–m* alternation acting as an accompaniment while *a* or *m* accents a melody. This fingerstyle technique is one of the many facets that makes the classical guitar so appealing.

Take Note

Be sure to keep your left-hand fingers down on the fingerboard so that the melody notes ring for their complete duration. This will ensure a *legato*, or smooth, melody line. In the right hand, alternation is paramount to creating the illusion that another guitar is churning away at the note G and filling in around the melody. Give a little accent to the melody, and keep the accompaniment and bass softer so that a hierarchy of voices is created. Presto! You sound like three instruments: melody, accompaniment, and bass!

We can thank Giuliani for inventing the system of notation that makes it possible to illustrate polyphony for the guitar. By changing the direction of stems and incorporating rests, he was able to convey the distinction between melody, inner voices, and bass on a single staff. In "Andantino," notice that the up-stems define the melody while the down-stems clarify the bass and accompaniment. Measure 20 incorporates a rest on the third beat so that the melody stops sounding and allows the accompaniment to ring through. This system is used in all guitar music.

TIP

The opening statement could be played by repeating *p* and *i* throughout the first section, but a more useful way would be to alternate *i* and *m* on the melody with *p* covering the bass. This is indicated with the *m* in parentheses as a suggested alternate fingering.

FUN FACT

In addition to being a virtuoso guitarist, Mauro Giuliani was also a fine cellist, which afforded him the distinct honor of playing at the premier of his friend Ludwig van Beethoven's 7th symphony.

Andantino

Mauro Giuliani

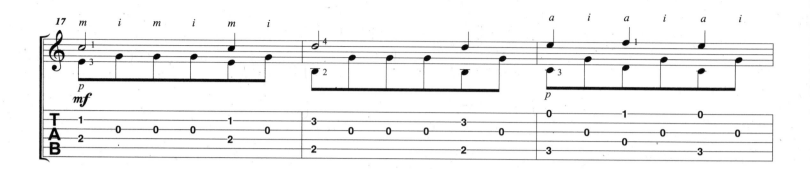

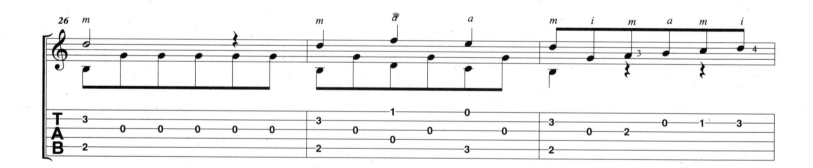

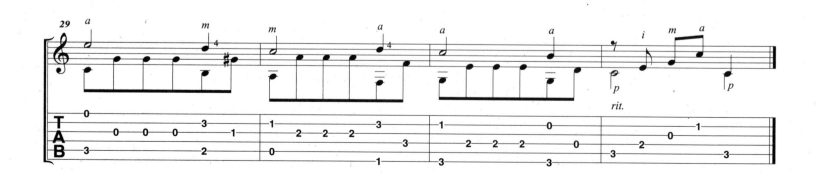

Españoleta
Gaspar Sanz (1640–1710)

Key Thoughts

When Spanish guitarist Gaspar Sanz composed "Españoleta" as part of his three-volume work titled *Instrucción de Música sobre la Guitarra Española*, he wrote it for a *baroque* guitar (from the era between 1600 to 1750) that was quite different from today's instrument. Though tuned in intervals of fourths, it had only five sets of strings, called *courses*, similar to today's 12-string guitar. Little did he know that this piece would become a link to today's modern classical guitar when Joaquin Rodrigo used it as the second movement theme of his famous guitar concerto *Fantasia para un Gentilhombre*.

Take Note

So far in this book, the left-hand fingerings have stayed in the open position. In "Españoleta," the fingerings are still primarily in the open position, but at measure 6, the 1st finger plays F on the 3rd fret, putting you squarely into the 3rd position. This is necessary because we will have to reach to the A on the 5th fret with the 4th finger and reserve the 2nd finger to play the G. Taking note of these details will become increasingly important as you progress through the book, since later pieces will be impossible to play if you don't notice the left-hand fingering.

A unique characteristic of baroque music was the advent of *ornamentation*; a baroque musician would first play through the selection stating the melody as written and then improvise and decorate the melody with musical ornaments on the repeat. This is similar to how a jazz musician plays the head of a piece true to the melody before proceeding to improvise upon it. The use of ornamentation is illustrated on the provided recording of this piece (though perhaps a bit overdone, for effect), and the various types of ornaments are marked and named in the music. Note that fingerings for both hands will change due to the ornaments. Although the scope of this book doesn't allow us to thoroughly convey this vast subject, it is fun to improvise on this melody the second time around and be introduced to the beauty of ornamentation. If this concept seems too complex for you at this time, just enjoy playing the beautiful melody as written. Remember, though, that you can use the TNT software to slow the music down to make it easier to play.

FUN FACT

Sanz was appointed "Instructor of Guitar" to Don Juan (John of Austria), the illegitimate son of Spanish King Phillip IV and the famous actress Maria La Calderona. Don Juan was the only recognized natural son of King Phillip and was therefore trained for military and political life. In 1677, he orchestrated a coup and took over the Spanish Monarchy. Guitar players in high places!

GUITAR GODS

GASPAR SANZ was not only a master of Spanish baroque guitar, but also an organist, poet, author, composer, and priest. A highly educated man who received his bachelor's degree in theology from the University of Salamanca, his great passion for music was secondary only to his devotion to God. Sanz traveled to Italy to study music with leading Italian figures such as Caresana, Colista, Ziani, and Benevoli, and his three-volume work *Instrucción de Música sobre la Guitarra Española*, written in *baroque tablature*, established him as the leading guitar authority of his day.

The most common ornaments, which you will see in this piece, are shown here.

Symbol	Name	Description	Example
᷇	upper mordent	A rapid alternation between the written note and its upper neighboring note in the key. Though not stylistic of this period, it is still fun to play.	From measure 4: 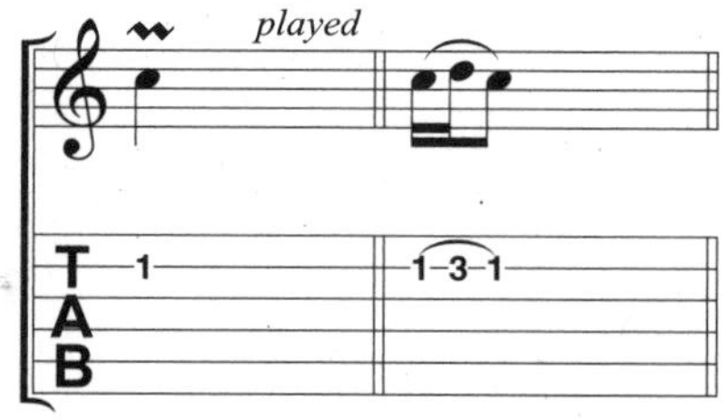
᷆	lower mordent	A rapid alternation between the written note and its lower neighboring note in the key.	From measure 2: 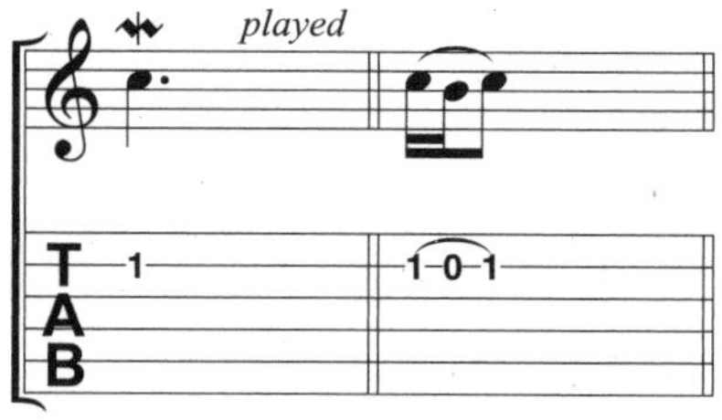
(♯) ᷤ	sharped mordent	Modifies a lower mordent to be a sharped note as opposed to a note that is a member of the key.	From measure 14: 
♪	appoggiatura	Meaning "to lean upon," a decorative note that displaces the main note and then resolves to it. To play the appoggiatura in measure 23, play the low A, E, and G♯ together, then casually resolve the G♯ to the A.	From measure 23: 
♪	acciaccatura	Meaning "to crush," a quick ornamental note played on the beat just before the main note. Play the ornament as if the decorative note is hot to the touch.	From measure 4: 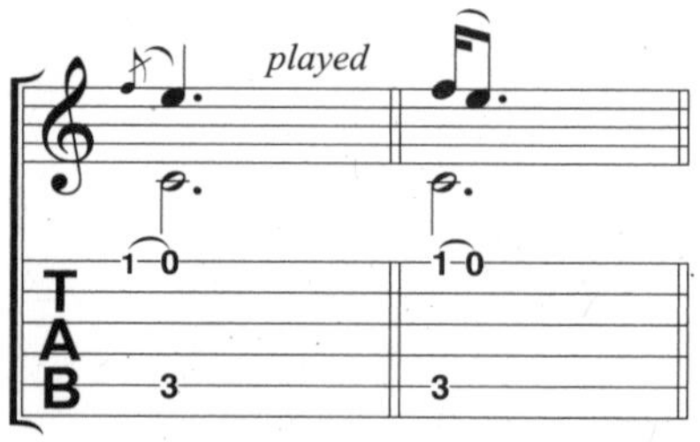
tr	trill	Rapid, successive alternation between the written note and its neighboring note either above or below. Generally, for music composed before the 1800s, start the trill with the upper neighbor and resolve downward. For music composed after 1800, start with the lower neighbor and resolve upward.	From measure 19: 

Españoleta

Gaspar Sanz

Menuett in A Minor
Johann Philipp Krieger (1649–1725)

Written in the baroque period, this menuett was probably first composed for keyboard rather than guitar, since Johann Philipp Krieger was the court organist and composer for Johanne Adolf I in Weißenfels, Germany, from 1680 to 1725. During this time, the musical court at Weißenfels became one of Germany's finest.

This piece should have a gentle, flowing feel, as if two instruments are having a calm dialogue. Be sure to allow the dotted half notes (such as in measures 2 and 4) to ring out for their full duration while the bass sounds its *counterpoint*. This will reinforce the illusion of two instruments playing at the same time. At first, playing at a slow tempo will help you develop the proper habits, but once you feel comfortable, a tempo of ♩ = 88 will be very nice. On the repeat, try adding some of the ornaments you learned in "Españoleta."

DEFINITION

Counterpoint refers to music with simultaneous independent voices.

With this work, we will now incorporate playing *p* simultaneously with *i*, *m*, or *a*. The fingering is still quite simple, but be sure that you still give sufficient follow-through whenever the thumb plays simultaneously with a finger. Watch out for the left-hand fingerings in measures 5 and 22—they don't follow standard open string fingering like the majority of the piece.

FUN FACT

Johann Philipp Krieger had a younger brother whose name was also Johann, and they came from a Nüremberg family of rug makers. Both were organists and composers, and the younger Johann succeeded his older brother as organist in Bayreuth, Germany, when Johann Philipp was promoted to Kapellmeister. This would make it easy in the modern world, since the name wouldn't have to be changed on the paycheck!

Menuett in A Minor

Johann Philipp Krieger

Menuett in D Major
Robert de Visée (1650–1725)

This menuett, like the preceding menuett in A minor, is also from the *baroque period*, and it provides a chance to dabble with an *altered tuning*, which is a different way of tuning the open strings of the guitar. The constant placement of bass notes on the downbeat of every measure gives the piece a real swaying kind of feel throughout. Be sure to allow those bass notes to ring for their complete duration, adding to the polyphonic effect of multiple instruments.

To extend the range and sound of the guitar, this piece uses *Drop D tuning*, meaning the 6th string is tuned a step lower to D. Notice the texture that is developed with this simple alteration. Drop D tuning is often indicated at the beginning of a piece with ⑥ = D.

While the earlier selections in this book are in open position, "Menuett in D Major" is in the second position. Any position on the guitar is determined by the 1st finger; if the 1st finger's responsibility is to cover the notes on the 2nd fret, then you are in second position. The fingers will then lay out from there; the 2nd finger on the 3rd fret, the 3rd finger on the 4th fret, and the 4th finger on the 5th fret. The fingerings are included in the music to help you with this concept.

TIP

Because this melody is linear in nature, be sure to alternate your right-hand fingers when playing scale-like passages. Just like walking left foot–right foot–left foot–right foot, alternating the fingers *i–m–i–m* creates a much smoother musical line. At first, you might have a tendency to want to repeat fingers, but once you replace this habit with alternation, your fluency will increase and your musical line will become very smooth.

GUITAR GODS

ROBERT DE VISÉE was an early singer-songwriter who composed songs for lute, guitar, theorbo, and viola da gamba. He was so prolific that, in 1719, he was named "Guitar Master of the King," serving as royal chamber musician for King Louis XIV of France and the official guitar tutor to nine-year-old Louis XV. Imagine having that on your resume—just don't stick around long enough that the job makes you lose your head.

Menuett in D Major

Robert de Visée

Exercise No. 18, Op. 35
Fernando Sor (1778–1839)

Key Thoughts

After publishing the instructional pieces *12 Studies*, Op. 6 and *12 Studies*, Op. 29, Fernando Sor set out to publish easier selections with *24 Progressive Lessons*, Op. 31. When students still found these selections too difficult, he published *24 Exercises*, Op. 35. Sor commented that, in his earlier studies and lessons, he should have "devoted to the pupil the attention which I gave to the music." It was at this point that he went from being a virtuoso guitarist to being a teacher, and opus 35 was born. Exercise no. 18, from this collection, focuses not only on right-hand development, but also on the forming of simple chords in the left hand.

Take Note

In this etude, the focus on right-hand development is fluency when alternating between the *m* and *a* fingers. Notice that the majority of *movement forms* (the specific motions you make to play the guitar) in the right hand have *i* and *m* moving sympathetically or together, while the majority of melodic notes are played with *a* alternating with *m*. Be sure to watch the dynamic balance of *a* with *p* so that the bass does not overwhelm the melody. Perhaps go back to page 8 and practice the alternation exercise with *a* and *m* to reinforce this movement.

As the *a* finger sounds the melodic line in this etude, it is important to hold down the associated left-hand finger for each note. When successfully executed, this will create a very legato melody that rings over the inner-voice chord changes. You will create the illusion of two guitars: a melody guitar and a *comping* guitar ("comp" being short for "accompaniment"). Pay special attention to the left-hand fingerings, and take note of some of the familiar open position chord forms that are used in this piece. Also, notice any right-hand fingerings in parentheses, which indicate other possible fingering options for you to consider.

TIP

In measure 7, notice the sign B II ⑤ above the second beat. If you haven't played a *barre chord* before, your 1st finger will extend across the fret to apply pressure to all the strings. In this case, your 1st finger will extend across the 2nd fret, as indicated by the Roman numeral II, and will extend to the 5th string, indicated by the number ⑤ in a circle.

FUN FACT

"Op." is short for the Latin word *opus*, which means "work," "labor," or "work of art." In the 19th century, opus numbers were assigned to music of similar composition, such as etudes or preludes. Opus numbers were assigned primarily to published works, so if no opus number exists for a piece, the work might not have been published during the composer's lifetime and may be categorized with "WoO," meaning "without opus."

Exercise No. 18, Op. 35

Fernando Sor

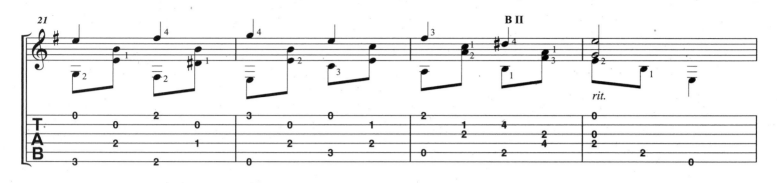

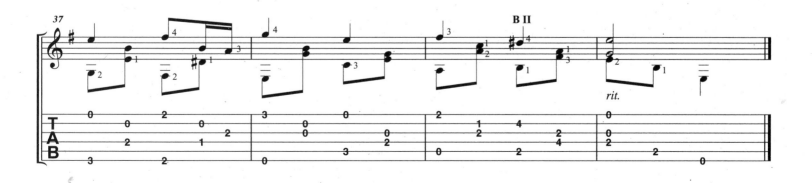

Exercise No. 17, Op. 35
Fernando Sor (1778–1839)

This melodic exercise from opus 35 provides a lesson in maintaining hierarchy among single lines. The notes with up-stems indicate the melodic line, while the notes with down-stems generally represent the accompaniment. Make sure the melody is legato (smooth), and that the melody has more presence than the supporting accompaniment.

Pay special attention to the left-hand fingerings throughout, and especially notice the B II sign at measures 2, 16, and 24, where the index finger extends to the 4th string. Also, notice how the fingers share responsibility, or "cover" for each other. For example, in measure 3, the 3rd finger has just finished holding the G, so successive notes are then covered by the 4th, then 1st, then 2nd fingers. This minimizes the less-desirable situation of hopping with repeated fingers. Granted, when playing chords, you have no choice but to hop fingers, but in situations where this can be avoided, by all means do so. Having fingers cover for each other smooths out the line and makes it easier to play.

TIP

Take a moment to play the melodic line (stems up) by itself to clearly hear how it evolves throughout the piece.

GUITAR GODS

FERNANDO SOR was born in Barcelona, Spain, and was considered one the greatest guitarists of his time. He achieved wide-spread fame across England, Germany, Poland, Spain, Russia, and France, and was the first and only guitarist to perform with the London Philharmonic during its first 100 years of existence. But early in his life, he was a captain in the Spanish army. In 1808, he helped defend Spain against an invasion by none other than Napoleon Bonaparte and the French Army. Fortunately for all us guitarists, he abandonded the military life of sword and cannon for the artistic life of fret and string…and canon.

Exercise No. 17, Op. 35

Fernando Sor

Exercise No. 22, Op. 35
Fernando Sor (1778–1839)

Key Thoughts

A melodic line is woven throughout this arpeggio exercise from Sor's opus 35. The up-stems depict the melody, and the down-stems are the accompaniment. The *p–i–m–i* arpeggio is the engine that drives this lovely piece.

Take Note

The **HB I** sign in measures 7 and 39 indicates a *hinge barre* at the 1st fret. A hinge barre uses the extended index finger to "hinge" on a note prior to placing the barre, which allows the barre to be prepared early and seamlessly placed in the next measure. Imagine the difficulty in measure 7, for example, if you used the pad of your 1st finger on the E♯ and then quickly extended the barre to play the F♯ major chord. With the hinge barre, the base of the extended index finger "hinges" on the E♯ to allow the adjacent B note to ring, and then easily lies down into the barre II to play the F♯ chord. This is demonstrated in the following photos.

Hinge barre from the base of the index finger.

Hinge barre leads to standard barre.

Note that a hinge barre can also hinge the other way, from the tip of the finger. This will allow a bass note to sound while open upper strings ring before hinging down to the barre chord.

Hinge barre from the tip of the index finger.

Hinge barre leads to standard barre.

TIP

When a passage is difficult, first identify the movement form that is giving you trouble and then do an *isolation*, meaning you will repeat the troublesome movement form by itself six, seven, eight, or more times until you're comfortable with its execution. For example, if the hinge barre is difficult for you to execute, isolate the E♯ in measure 7 as it moves to the F♯ in measure 8. Do this a number of times until moving from the hinge barre to the standard barre feels comfortable—or until you drive anyone who's listening absolutely nuts!

GUITAR GODS

FERNANDO SOR was a double threat—both great performer and composer. His compositions for the guitar span 10 volumes, and his "Variations on a Theme by Mozart" is one of the most famous virtuoso pieces for guitar. But perhaps Sor's most valuable contributions are his collections of exercises, lessons, and studies that provide material with beautiful melodies for beginning and intermediate guitarists. In 1830, he published his guitar method *Methode pour la Guitare* in French, which is still available today. His works progress to opus 63, and his works without opus include 33 arias, 26 seguidillas (romantic songs), 2 operas, 7 ballets, and 3 symphonies. You may be surprised to learn that Sor tended to be a sarcastic character, dedicating works to "whoever wants them" or, in the case of six short and easy pieces, to "the person with the least patience."

Exercise No. 22, Op. 35

Fernando Sor

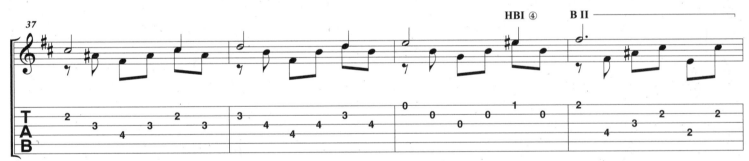

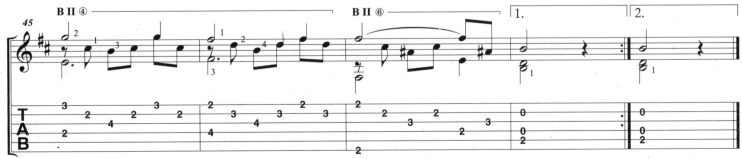

Minuet in G Major
Johann Sebastian Bach (1685–1750)

This famous minuet, originally written for keyboard, is part of the *Notebook for Anna Magdalena Bach*, a compilation of music assembled in 1725 by Johann Sebastian Bach and his second wife, Anna Magdalena. Containing works by Bach and other composers of the era, this notebook was a greatest-hits collection for the Bach family and a teaching tool for the children. It provides a snapshot of how it would sound to live in an 18th-century musical household. (An 18th-century style wig is not necessary to play this piece!)

Pay special attention to the left- and right-hand fingerings indicated throughout the piece; following them will make the music easy to play because the notes lie under the hands. At measure 7, be sure your elbow comes in towards your torso to facilitate the positioning of the F♯ on the 4th string and the D on the 5th string. The arm and hand should "yield" to the pull of the fingers when positioning is tricky. Remember this especially when the 4th finger must be placed on lower strings while the 1st and 2nd fingers are on higher strings.

TIP

To give this selection the flowing feel it deserves, be sure to alternate the right-hand fingers as indicated. It's a good idea to warm up with some scales and reinforce the habit of *i–m* alternation before you begin practicing the piece. Doing this on a daily basis will ultimately cause the alternation technique to become a natural habit you perform without having to think about it.

FUN FACT

Although this work is attributed to Johann Sebastian Bach, research has revealed that it was actually written by Christian Petzold, a baroque organist and composer who resided in Dresden, Germany. The Bachs admired the piece so much that they included it in their collection of favorites, the *Notebook for Anna Magdalena Bach,* and historians throughout the years mistakenly identified it as J. S. Bach's composition. Considering that Petzold's roster of compositions is much smaller than Bach's, strictly from the numbers it's only fair to give Petzold his props.

Minuet in G Major

Johann Sebastian Bach

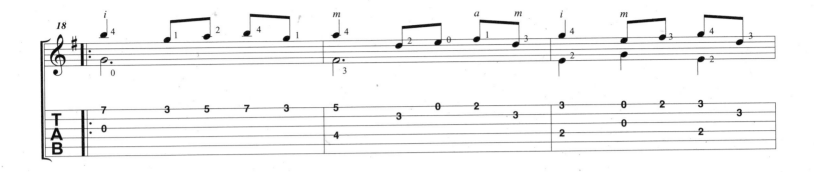

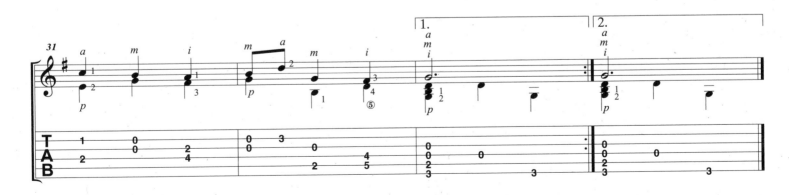

Minuet in G Minor
(transposed)
Johann Sebastian Bach (1685–1750)

Key Thoughts

This piece is another keyboard selection from the *Notebook for Anna Magdalena Bach*, but it has been transposed to A minor for our guitar transcription to fit a bit easier under the hand. (Like the previous minuet, it was mistakenly credited by historians through the years as the work of Johann Sebastian Bach and later discovered to be the composition of Christian Petzold.) The simple structure of the minuet presents a good opportunity to experiment with changes in tonal color—it is the ability of the classical guitar to produce such a wide pallet of color that prompted the great Andrés Segovia to refer to the guitar as a "mini orchestra."

Take Note

Like the preceding minuet in G major, both the first and second sections of this piece (referred to as the **A** and **B** sections) have repeats. To keep things interesting, it might be nice to try a "color" change, meaning a variation in tone, when stating the part the second time. Color changes are created by moving your right hand either closer to the fingerboard to produce a warmer sound, or closer to the bridge to create a brighter sound. Playing closer to the fingerboard is referred to as *sul tasto*, and playing closer to the bridge is called *sul ponticello*. When you proceed to the repeat of a section, move your right hand toward the desired color, and listen to how it suggests a different instrument of the "guitar orchestra."

TIP

If this piece were in the original key of G minor, it would be very fitting to play the G major minuet on page 49, then proceed to this G minor minuet, and then play the G major piece again. This would create a little multi-movement set that shares a common *tonic* (the note G) but different *modality* (major and minor). You can still play this set with the minuet transposed to A minor—it's just not as neat and clean from a theoretical standpoint. But hey, what the heck—go have fun with your first multi-movement selection!

GUITAR GODS

ANDRÉS SEGOVIA (1893–1987) gave his first public performance in 1909 at the age of 16, and is credited with almost single-handedly bringing the classical guitar from the salons and the music rooms of family homes into the concert halls of the world. Performing well into his eighties, his performances and recordings have enthralled generations of fans and inspired scores of people to pursue the classical guitar. One of Segovia's signature attributes was his ability to create a wide pallet of tonal color on the guitar. Take some time and refer to the suggested listening in Appendix C to experience what so many have found to be an inspiration.

Minuet in G Minor
(transposed)

Johann Sebastian Bach

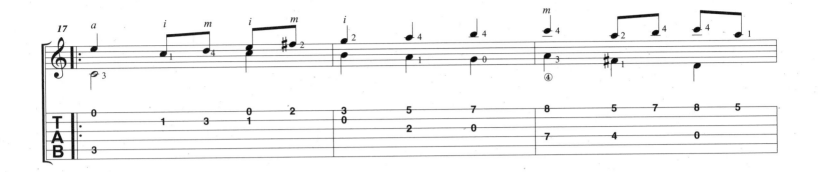

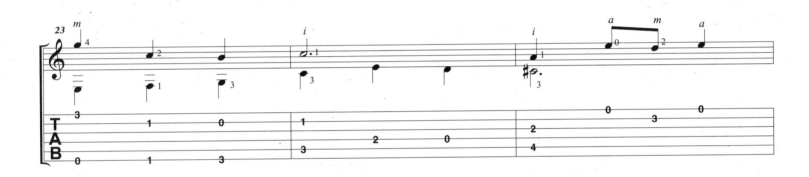

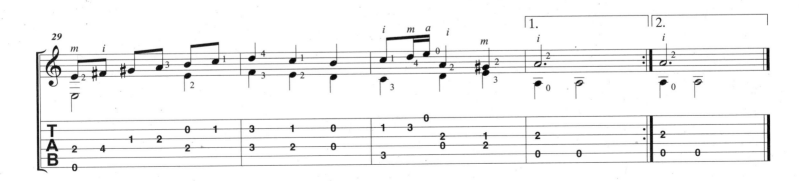

Etude in E Minor
Dionisio Aguado (1784–1849)

Key Thoughts

This *etude*, a piece that works on specific technique, will re-introduce you to the arpeggio. As you have learned, an arpeggio played on the classical guitar is a right-hand finger pattern performed while holding a chord with the left hand. A basis of folk-style fingerpicking, this technique incorporates sympathetic motion to organize the fingers in a flowing pattern. Fortunately, this etude stays in the open position for the left hand, making it a bit easier to learn and play and providing an opportunity to focus on the proper motion for the right-hand arpeggio.

Take Note

Although this etude is written with a *p–i–m–a–m–i* arpeggio, we are going to start off with a simpler *p–i–m–a* arpeggio that still works with the written music, then, we will practice a *p–a–m–i* arpeggio. The same chord progressions can be used as you begin applying sympathetic motion to create these right-hand patterns; you simply need to modify each *sextuplet* and play four sixteenth notes instead.

DEFINITION

Named for the French word meaning "study," an **etude** is a piece in which one will find a specific technical issue that is emphasized and applied. Thousands of etudes have been written for various instruments. The focus of this E minor etude is the development of proper form and sympathetic movement for arpeggios.

TIP

Remember that the fingers move together sympathetically, as a team: The pull of *i* pulls in *m*, and the pull of *m* pulls in *a*. The motion is the same as when playing a chord, but the sounding of each string is sequential. Although you may not yet fathom the importance of developing these movement forms, as you experience more music, you will realize that sympathetic movement is essential to smooth phrasing and a relaxed right hand. You will find elements of this in all pieces played.

![TNT icon] Playing the Arpeggio *p–i–m–a*

1/14 To begin the *p–i–m–a* arpeggio, place your hand as shown.

Setup for p–i–m–a arpeggio.

Sound the bass string with *p* first, followed by *i–m–a*.

Play bass note with p. *Play 3rd string with i.* *Play 2nd string with m.* *Play 1st string with a.*

When *p* sounds again, the fingers should extend to get ready to play another cycle. In essence, the fingers move together sympathetically, and *p* acts to reset the sympathetic fingers.

As p sounds again, the fingers extend together and reset.

As you learn the entire piece, continue developing fluency so that you feel comfortable playing the *p–i–m–a* arpeggio. Be sure to listen to the excerpt on track 14 of the CD.

Playing the Arpeggio *p–a–m–i*

1/15 Once you feel comfortable playing *p–i–m–a*, try playing with *p–a–m–i*. Listen to the excerpt on track 15 for clarification.

Setup for p-a-m-i arpeggio.

Play bass note with p.

Play 1st string with a.

Play 2nd string with m.

Play 3rd string with i.

As p sounds again, the fingers extend together and reset.

GUITAR GODS

DIONISIO AGUADO (1784–1849) was a Spanish classical guitarist, author, and composer. His treatise *Nuevo Metodo para Guitarra* (New Method for Guitar), published in 1843, was one of the first method books to create a technical foundation for classical guitarists. Although his guitar contemporaries composed music for various other instruments, Aguado wrote only for solo guitar and composed many works for the instrument.

Playing the Full Arpeggio *p–i–m–a–m–i*

With your mastery of *p–i–m–a* and *p–a–m–i*, you now have the building blocks to play the complete *p–i–m–a–m–i* arpeggio Aguado originally wrote.

Begin with *p–i–m* just as you did for the *p–i–m–a* arpeggio, but when *a* sounds, you must extend and reset *m* and *i* to prepare them to continue playing sympathetically and finish out the arpeggio. Then, when *p* sounds again, the fingers all reset to play another cycle. The following sequence of photos demonstrates the form.

Hand setup.

Play bass note with p.

Play 3rd string with i.

Play 2nd string with m.

Play 1st string with a, and reset m and i.

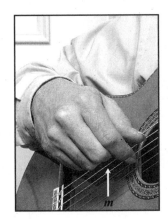

Play 2nd string with m.

Play 3rd string with i.

Play bass note with p, and reset the fingers.

Etude in E Minor

Dionisio Aguado

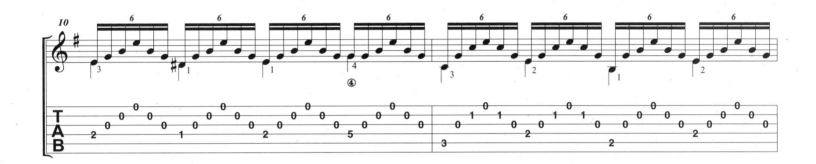

Saltarello
Anonymous

Key Thoughts

Born in Bassano, Italy, Oscar Chilesotti (1848–1916) first studied law but soon realized his love was music, particularly for lute. Although he lived during the middle of the romantic period, his heart was firmly rooted in the past, as one can tell from his works of musicology. Chilesotti uncovered hundreds of dances, madrigals, and arias written for lute throughout the 16th to 18th centuries, which he compiled into a series of publications known today as the Chilesotti Lute Collection. This *saltarello* is from that body of work, though the composer is unknown.

Take Note

This selection uses *Drop D tuning*, which was introduced in "Menuett in D Major." The key to executing this piece is right-hand *i–m* alternation, which will allow the sixteenth notes to sound crisp and smooth. Also, notice how the melody and bass lines converge in measures 40, 44, 46, and 52, requiring that you play the bass note D on the 5th string at the 5th fret to keep the two lines sounding as independent parts.

At the end of the saltarello, there is a series of notes with diamond-shaped heads called *harmonics*. A harmonic is a soft, ringing, bell-like tone created by just lightly touching the string directly over the indicated fret brass (the little bar of brass on the neck that defines the fret). For example, to play a harmonic at the 12th fret, place your left-hand finger on a string just over the piece of brass at the 12th fret—don't push the string down, just touch it. Then, sound the string with a finger of the right hand and lift the fretting finger. When done correctly, you will hear a beautiful, bell-like sound.

Just touch a string lightly over the fret brass to finger a harmonic.

Lightly touch multiple strings with a barre to get multiple harmonics.

TIP

The bass line of this saltarello mimics the sound of a string instrument called a *hurdy-gurdy*. Turning a crank on the hurdy-gurdy produces a continuous drone-like bass while the melody is played on a small keyboard. Because this piece has two such distinct musical parts, you may find it easier to practice the melody alone first to focus on proper fingerings, and then, when comfortable, incorporate the bass line to complete the effect.

FUN FACT

Most of the works in the Chilesotti Lute Collection are anonymous compositions, meaning the composer is unknown; however, some of the pieces have been credited to Vincenzo Galilei, the father of the great 17th-century astronomer Galileo Galilei.

64

Saltarello

Anonymous

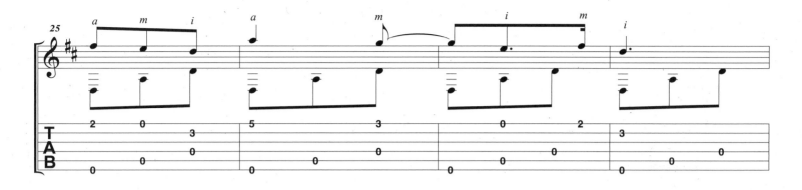

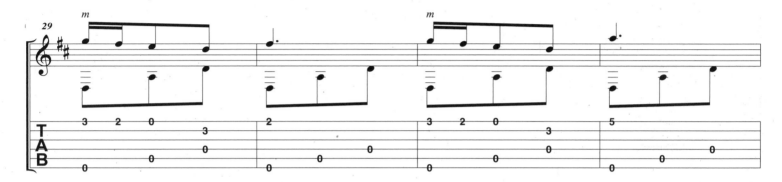

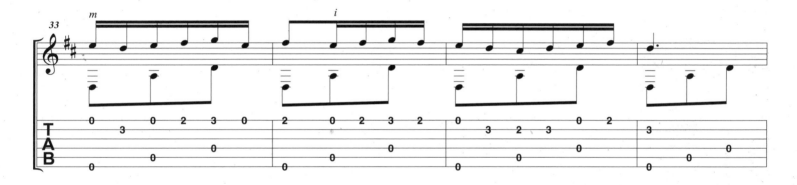

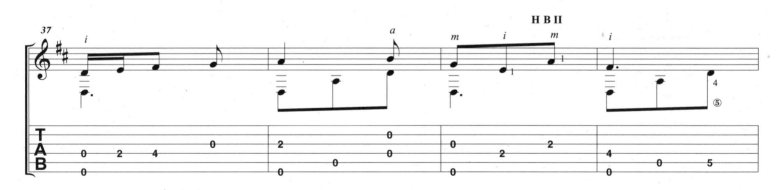

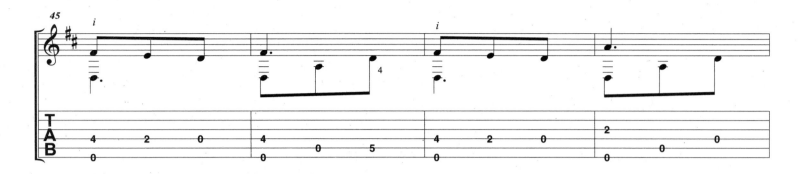

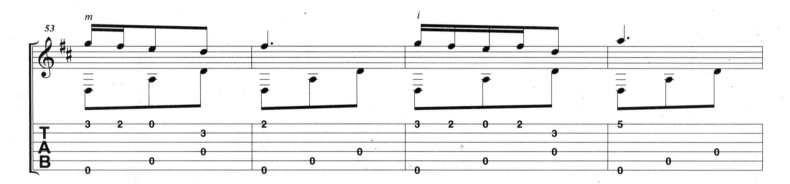

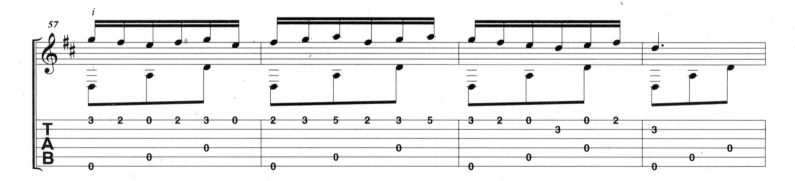

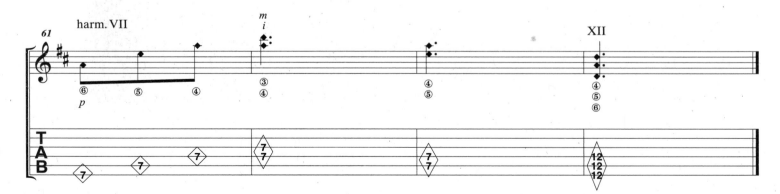

Spanish Romance (Romanza)

Anonymous

The haunting melody of this popular piece from classical guitar repertoire is one of the most-requested selections at parties, weddings, and concert encores. Known by various titles but with no confirmed composer or date of composition, "Spanish Romance" is representative of the popular style and form of the late 19th-century parlour music of Spain.

The three-part form of "Spanish Romance" can be described as **A–B–A**. The first section (**A**) begins in the key of E minor and modulates to E major, the *parallel major*, for the **B** section (measure 18) before returning to the **A** section in E minor to close out the piece.

This piece uses an *a–m–i* arpeggio, which is one of the five *arpeggios without p*. Although *p* is used, it merely accents the downbeat played with *a* and therefore is not actually a member of the arpeggio. Fingers *a* and *m* move sympathetically as a pair, and *i* and *m* will actually alternate as *i* acts as a reset finger for the sympathetic pair. The following photos illustrate the form.

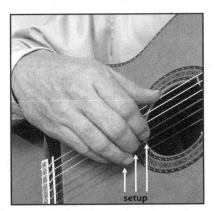

Set up your right hand as usual.

Sound the 1st string with a.

Pull in m sympathetically to sound the 2nd string.

As i sounds the 3rd string, a and m move together to prepare for the next arpeggio.

Once you are comfortable with the arpeggio, practice sounding p simultaneously with a.

Spanish Romance (Romanza)

Anonymous

Lágrima
("Tear")
Francisco Tárrega (1852–1909)

Francisco Tárrega was inspired to compose this piece in 1881 while touring in London, where he was lonely for home and not particularly happy with the weather or surroundings England had to offer. After a concert, some fans noticed his discomfort and suggested that he channel his sadness into a new composition. He titled the expression of his sorrow "Lágrima," meaning a "tear," and it is one of his most beautiful melodies.

The repeating *motif*—a two eighth-note figure with a high note falling to a low note—represents the falling of tears. It begins with the first two eighth notes and occurs throughout the piece to convey the sadness Tárrega was feeling. The top of each pair is the melody, so connect them *legato*. Listen to the CD for clarification.

The beautiful melody of "Lágrima" is characteristic of the heartwarming sounds of the romantic period. To play this piece stylistically, don't be afraid to use a lot of *rubato*. Rubato means "robbing of time" and indicates that the tempo should slightly speed up and slow down at times to give the melody a feeling of give-and-take, as if it is breathing. As the melody ascends, allow the tempo to speed up a bit, and when the top note is reached, relax the tempo to softly land on the lower notes. Listen to the provided recording of this piece to get a sense of rubato; notice that the tempo is not constant, but rather a push and pull of time.

GUITAR GODS

FRANCISCO TÁRREGA is considered to be the father of the 20th-century guitar. As a boy, he showed great promise mimicking his father's *flamenco* guitar playing, and at the age of 10 he was sent to Barcelona to study guitar and piano. With a propensity for a free lifestyle, the teenage Francisco would often run away to play in bars, coffeehouses, and restaurants (even going so far as to join a gang of gypsies and eventually end up hundreds of miles away in Valencia). At the age of 17, he traveled to Seville in hopes of buying a new guitar from Antonio de Torres, a master guitar maker considered to be the Stradivarius of guitar luthiers. Upon hearing Tárrega play, Torres reconsidered his decision to sell the boy a lesser-sounding instrument, and instead, he offered his own personal instrument of superior quality and tone. The "father of modern guitar making" had given his instrument to be played by the "father of modern guitar," and as Tárrega gained fame performing throughout Europe, he established the guitar as a serious recital instrument. His genius was passed on to future generations through his compositions as well as his teaching of such future greats as Emilio Pujol and Miguel Llobet.

Lágrima
("Tear")

Francisco Tárrega

Prelude
Francisco Tárrega (1852–1909)

At a very young age, Francisco Tárrega's eyesight was permanently impaired by a rare infection. His first two music teachers, Eugeni Ruiz and Manuel González, were both blind. Perhaps this tragic disability became an asset, enabling him to compose and perform music so that he could hear the beauty that he could not see. This prelude is a stunning example.

This piece moves all over the neck using the upper register of the instrument, which creates a music box quality. Be sure to notice the harmonic on beat 2 of measure 2 that adds to the effect. Also, note the indication for Drop D tuning at the beginning of the music.

TIP

In measure 3, an open E allows a smooth transition from a high position on the neck to a lower position. Using an open note in this way is a good idea when you need to make a shift but don't want to interrupt the musical phrase.

FUN FACT

Tárrega composed 78 pieces to help expand the classical guitar repertoire. His most famous works are "Capricho Arabe," "Gran Vals," "Danza Mora," and the tremolo selection "Recuerdos de la Alhambra." The latter piece was used in the soundtrack for the film *The Killing Fields,* and "Gran Vals" is said to be the theme used for the Nokia ringtone.

Prelude

Francisco Tárrega

⑥ = D

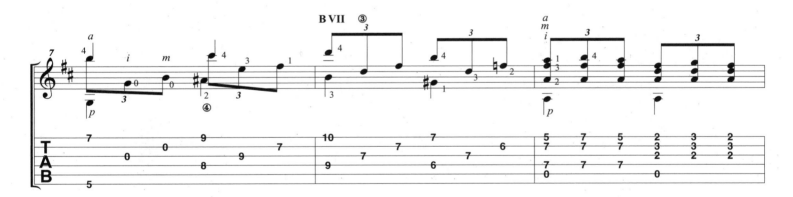

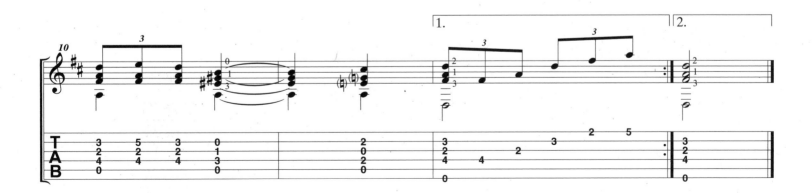

Etude No. 3, Op. 60, in A Major
Matteo Carcassi (1792–1853)

Key Thoughts

This etude introduces the use of two arpeggios to create a dialogue of melodies between different registers on the guitar. The *a–i–m* arpeggio sets the main melody in motion on the 1st string (primarily), while the *p–i–m* arpeggio creates a response in the bass. This creates the illusion of not just one, but rather two instruments having a dialogue, much like a violin and cello might interact in an orchestra.

Take Note

The proper form for both arpeggios used in this study piece is critical for a smooth and articulate sound. The *p–i–m* arpeggio is very much like the *p–i–m–a* arpeggio in the "Etude in E Minor" by Aguado on page 56, but without the *a* finger playing. Remember to move *a* and *c* sympathetically with *m*.

For the *a–i–m* arpeggio, make sure that *a* and *m* are moving together at all times and that an alternation is occurring between *i* and *m*. Putting both arpeggios together will produce the sequence shown below.

Combining Arpeggios *p–i–m* and *a–i–m*

p

i

m

a

i

m

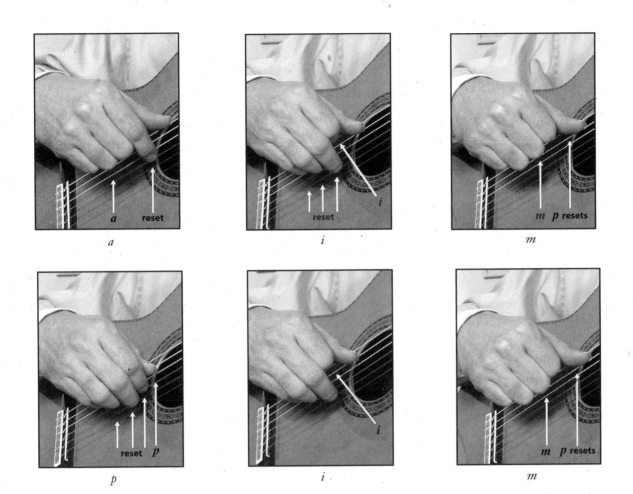

a   *i*   *m*

p   *i*   *m*

TIP

It would be wise to practice the two arpeggios separately before combining them in this piece. Take the first beat of measure 1 and continue to repeat the *p–i–m* arpeggio as an exercise until it begins to feel fluent. Also, take the second and third beat of the first measure and repeat it to reinforce the habit of the *a–i–m* arpeggio. By repeating an easy left-hand segment, you can focus on proper execution of the right hand. This will make matters much easier when you finally combine them to play the piece.

GUITAR GODS

From 1810 to 1840, **MATTEO CARCASSI** performed concerts of great virtuosity in some of the most culturally rich cities of Europe. He gained tremendous fame in London, Paris, Italy, and Germany, both as a performer and a teacher. He stopped performing in 1840, and after all his travels settled in Paris where he lived until his death in 1853. His obituary stated that, "He had made of France, which he had served as a soldier, his adopted and favorite country."

Etude No. 3, Op. 60, in A Major

Matteo Carcassi

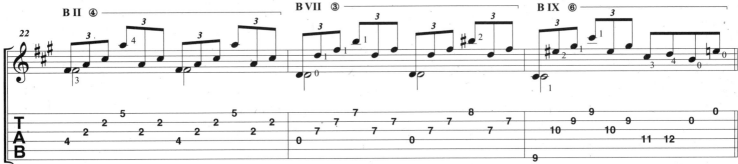

Etude No. 7, Op. 60, in A Minor
Matteo Carcassi (1792–1853)

Key Thoughts

Like "Etude No. 3," this etude is from Carcassi's collection of *25 Etudes*, Op. 60 that was published around 1836. Carcassi's etudes combine techniques needed by the classical guitarist with lovely musical ideas that keep the pieces relevant and enjoyable to this day. "Etude No. 7" was written to introduce the concept of *tremolo*. This technique has the repeating note A sustained on top of a moving bass-line melody. The fingers play an *a–m–i* arpeggio movement, but this time repeating the A on a single string, and the thumb has the duty of playing the moving bass line. The resulting arpeggio is *p–a–m–i*, but *a–m–i* is on the same string—in this case, initially the 3rd string.

Take Note

Make sure that fingers *a*, *m*, and *i* are moving sympathetically, as shown in the following pictures. Remember the thumb will reset the sympathetic group of fingers.

Playing the Arpeggio *p–a–m–i*

Prepare p on the 5th string with a on the 3rd string.

p

a

m

i

As p plays, a resets.

TIP

When not performing a tremolo, the rule for the right-hand fingering in this work is to let the *a* finger cover the 1st string, the *m* finger play the 2nd string, and the *i* finger play the 3rd string. In places where this doesn't apply, fingerings have been written in.

GUITAR GODS

Italian composer, teacher, and author **MATTEO CARCASSI** was regarded as one of the great virtuoso guitarists of his time. Today, he is best remembered for his guitar method *Méthode Complète pour la Guitare,* Op. 59, and his *25 Etudes,* Op. 60, which are still frequently visited by today's guitarists. Carcassi wrote enough music to have 74 opus numbers assigned, but 22 of the works appear to be lost.

Etude No. 7, Op. 60, in A Minor

Matteo Carcassi

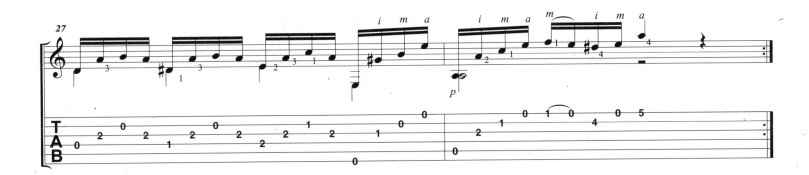

Pavan No. 1
Luys Milán (1500–1561)

With "Pavan No. 1," we go all the way back to the origins of guitar and tablature. Luys Milán refers to this piece as a "fantasie that resembles the air and composition of the pavans which are played in Italy." This was the first pavan of six that were in Milán's popular publication *El Maestro*, an instructional book printed in December of 1536 for self-taught players of the *vihuela*. An ancestor of both the guitar and the baroque guitar, the vihuela had six *courses* (double strings) tuned GCFADG, and it was played with the nail using techniques similar to those used for lute. The tablature was Milán's own system, which had the highest string on the top of the TAB staff and used numbers to represent the fret positions—sounds familiar, doesn't it? To simulate the sound of the vihuela's shorter strings, you'll need to place a *capo* on the 3rd fret of the guitar, which will make the tuning very close to the open strings of the vihuela.

DEFINITION

A **capo** is a device that is placed around the neck of the guitar to raise the pitch of the strings, eliminating the need to continuously hold a barre at that fret.

This *pavan* (a slow and stately dance form) exemplifies the right-hand organization that was discussed in the beginning of this book. If you're playing chords, then the right hand is using *p* with *i–m–a* moving sympathetically. If scale passages are being played, then some form of alternation is going to be employed. Once again, you are either moving sympathetically or alternating—one or the other.

One other little point: Pay special attention to the left-hand fingering so that the *polyphony* is not disturbed. For example, in measure 7, the 1st finger is holding the A while the 2nd finger reaches over the top of it to play the E. Seems awkward, but once you get it, you will see that it allows the A to ring for its full two beats, creating a beautiful *suspension* over the E chord that will then resolve to the G♯.

TIP

With the capo at the 3rd fret, play the notes on the guitar as if the capo is the nut. Don't get confused—you read and play the music as if the capo wasn't there, but the music will sound up a minor third in the key of C minor. If you want, you can take it a step farther with a slight *altered tuning*, and lower the 3rd string one half step from G to F♯ (referenced with no capo). This would now give you the true vihuela tuning with the capo at the 3rd fret. Realize you have to change the left-hand fingerings to accommodate this. Another point to keep in mind is that if you ever try to play lute or vihuela tablature, which is available, you would have to adjust your guitar this way or things will sound very strange.

GUITAR GODS

LUYS MILÁN was born of noble parents around 1500 in Valencia, Spain. Living in the Spanish Renaissance, he was employed as a musician for the Valencian ducal court and went on to compose works for the vihuela. Milán is credited with many "firsts" in the world of guitar. His publication *El Maestro* was the first book for vihuela ever printed on a printing press. Much like the Internet today, the printing press in 1536 was a very powerful tool for spreading information very quickly, which explains why Milán's system of tablature stood the test of time even though French, German, and Italian systems already existed. Milán's system is also closest to what modern music uses today. He is also known for verbose tempo indications; where today we would say "Allegro," Milán has written a tempo of "Rather quick tactus."

You could say that Milán went on to be a sort of gossip writer with his final 1561 publication *El Cortesano*, which contained no music but gave an entertaining behind-the-scenes look at life as a musician in a royal court. It was a sort of renaissance "Spinal Tap," if you will—but his vihuela did not go to 11.

Pavan No. 1

Capo 3rd fret to match recording.

Luys Milán

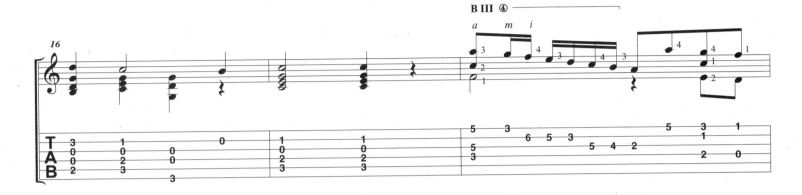

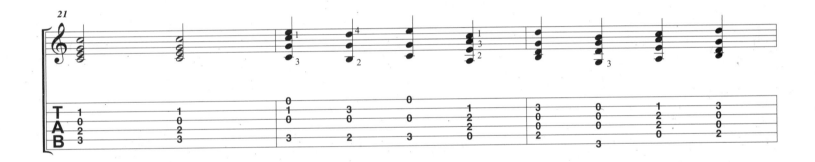

El Noi de la Mare
Catalan Folk Song

Key Thoughts

A traditional Catalan Christmas carol, "El Noi de la Mare" translates as "The Son of Mary." Many European countries sing this song at the holiday season, and its beautiful melody is truly inspiring—so much so that many instrumental versions have been made.

Take Note

This arrangement starts out quite simple and proceeds to higher levels of complexity with each repetition throughout the **A–A–B–A** form. If certain movement forms are too complex, just use the simpler voicing, and scale the difficulty up or down to suit your ability. In either case, it is a beautiful composition.

Legato is the word here; allow the melody to sing smoothly over the top of the lush harmonies supporting it. Keep each melody finger planted on the fingerboard so the notes flow together.

Also, notice the *artificial harmonic* in measure 59, indicated with A.H. To execute this, fret the note A with the left hand as usual; then, just barely touch the string over the fret brass with the right-hand *i* finger 12 frets up from the fretted note and sound the harmonic with the right-hand *a* finger. A high, bell-like sound will be produced, just like a natural harmonic.

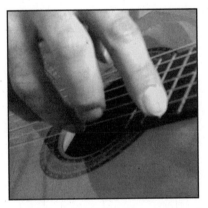

Playing an artificial harmonic using i to lightly touch the string and a to sound the note.

GUITAR GODS

Many guitarists have arranged this piece, including Miguel Llobet, Christopher Parkening, Aaron Shearer, and the great **ANDRÉS SEGOVIA** who use to close his concerts with this piece as the final encore. It is very easy to find numerous video performances online of Segovia playing this.

El Noi de la Mare

Catalan Folk Song

Greensleeves
Anonymous Elizabethan Folk Song

Key Thoughts

The beautiful folk song "Greensleeves" has stood the test of time and is one of music's most recognizable melodies. We know it was already famous in the Elizabethan period because Shakespeare refers to it in his 1602 comedic play *The Merry Wives of Windsor*, when the character Sir John Falstaff says, "Let the sky rain potatoes! Let it thunder to the tune of Greensleeves!" So, with that said, wait 'til it's thundering, then get your guitar, play "Greensleeves," and watch out for falling potatoes!

Take Note

This arrangement has a bit of a "new age" feel, so although our focus is on playing it on the classical guitar, it will work equally well on an acoustic steel-string guitar. Allow lots of string ringing since the minor 9th and major 7th chords add a haunting quality to the piece.

The melody and introduction are harmonized with *intervals* of 6ths. On the guitar, this creates an opportunity to put the two voices parallel to each other on the 1st and 3rd strings, such as in measures 1–4. Notice that, by doing so, the 3rd finger becomes a *glide finger* that guides the hand as it shifts up and down the neck. Keep the fingers in contact with the strings as a reference to where you are at all times. Just don't allow the underlying string to *gliss* as you shift, or it will become too much and start sounding like a recording speeding up and slowing down.

Andante cantabile ♩ = 86

Both "Greensleeves" and "Guardame las Vacas" (also in this book) are in the form called a **romanesca**. A romanesca has four chords that continuously repeat to form a foundation over which one can improvise or create a variation. As you learn these pieces, identify the four chords and hear how they cycle underneath. This is the early ancestor to the concept of *theme and variation*, also found later in this book.

The following is an optional way to play measures 17 and 18. It's a bit tougher to reach, but worth it to get the support of the moving bass line.

GUITAR GODS

JOHN DOWLAND is probably the greatest musical star to come out of the Elizabethan era. This composer, singer, and lutenist set the tone for the artsy singer-songwriter that would come of age almost 400 years later in the 20th century. A prolific writer, Dowland composed some of the most memorable and popular melodies of his time, including "Come Heavy Sleep," "Flow My Tears," and those from "Lachrimae." His books of lute songs were arranged in a manner that allowed them to be performed with voice and lute or with other instrumentation, if so desired. His work even influenced the 20th-century composer Benjamin Britten when he wrote "Nocturnal" for guitar, based on "Come Heavy Sleep."

Greensleeves

Anonymous Elizabethan Folk Song
Arranged by Thomas Kikta

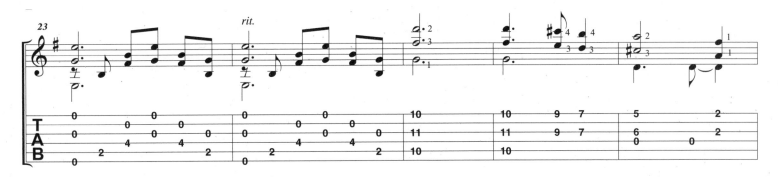

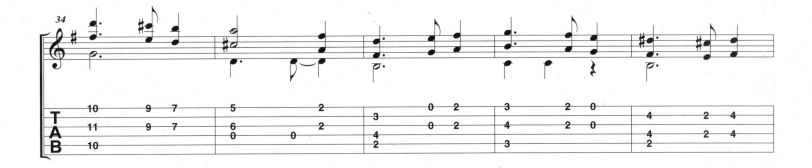

Leyenda
(simplified)
Isaac Albéniz (1860–1909)

When Isaac Albéniz wrote the piano piece "Leyenda" (originally titled "Prelude"), he was trying to capture the feel of Andalusian *flamenco* guitar music. He did this by imitating the characteristic *pedal tone*, a constantly sounding note, which a guitarist would sound along with the melody using an alternating thumb and finger technique. What better way to honor this piece than to play it on the guitar that inspired it! Also called "Asturias," this work was made famous for guitar by the great Andrés Segovia.

So far throughout the book, I have tried to stay true to the original scores and make matters easier by giving good fingerings and detailed instruction as to how to approach each piece. It is with this selection that we scrub those intentions. Not to offend the purists out there who will say we pillaged this masterpiece, but the original score probably would have frustrated you after about 16 measures. In this simplified arrangement, the original flow and sound of the work has been successfully maintained by simply revoicing the chords to make it lay under your hands a bit easier. Also, the more difficult aspects of the *adagio* section have been removed by having it *recapitulate* (repeat) from the beginning. If you never knew the original, this simplified arrangement should stand on its own just fine. But, with that being said, when your chops finally advance to the point that more advanced repertoire is feasible, then, by all means, go get a copy of the full transcription and go at it. Have fun—it's the kind of piece that sounds hard but is really rather easy once you get the hang of it.

The right-hand movement forms in "Leyenda" include a *p–m* alternation, a *p–i–m* arpeggio, and a *p–m–i* tremolo. Be sure to use sympathetic motion on the *i* and *m* fingers in the arpeggio and tremolo. The arpeggio movement is identical to the *p–i–m–a* arpeggio without using *a*, and the tremolo movement is identical to the *p–a–m–i* tremolo without using *a*. In both cases, be sure to allow *a* to go along for the ride and move sympathetically with *m* even though it will not sound a string. (Be sure *c* does the same. Don't let *c* stick out!)

TIP

At measure 17, a *thumb sweep* is used to play the two E's on the downbeats. The thumb sweeps both notes as the arpeggio follows. At first, it may help to tilt your hand outward slightly to assist the thumb sweep and then tilt it back in to complete the arpeggio. It's best not to do this if you don't have to, but sometimes it helps in the beginning.

For the left hand, the word is *power chord*. If you know your basic rock and roll barre chord, then this piece should be a cinch. Mostly, there are single notes played in 7th position, and then the downbeats are ultimately punctuated with full barre chords. To play these chords, the right hand will execute a *rasgueado* to give each one the impact it deserves.

DEFINITION

A **rasgueado** is a rapid sympathetic extending of right-hand fingers in the order *a–m–i* that is done so quickly it sounds like one "flammed" strum. To practice, start with your right hand in a closed fist. Then, extend each finger individually to strum across the strings with the back of the nail. Finally, practice extending the three fingers in one fluid motion, sympathetically, and the explosive sound of the rasgueado is created.

Start the rasgueado with the fingers closed like a fist.

Extend a, m, and i sympathetically.

FUN FACT

Albéniz first wrote "Leyenda" in 1892 as part of a three-movement work titled *Cantos de España*. Two years after the composer's death, his publisher released it as part of a "new" work called *Suite Española,* which depicts aural snapshots of different regions of Spain. The first guitar transcription, however, is believed to have been done by Francisco Tárrega.

Leyenda
(simplified)

Isaac Albéniz
Arranged by Thomas Kikta

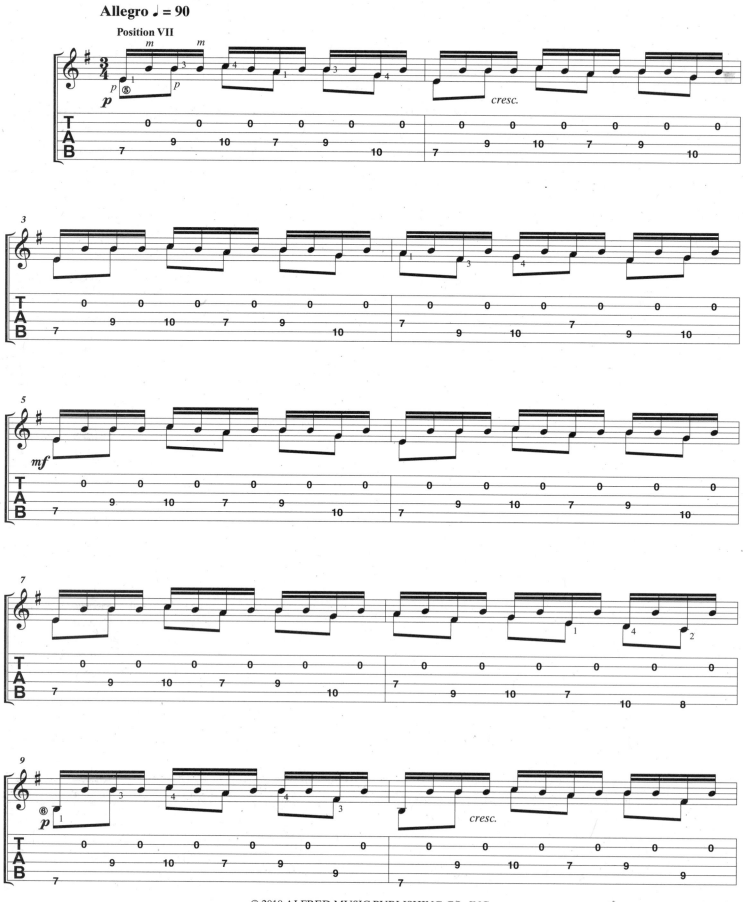

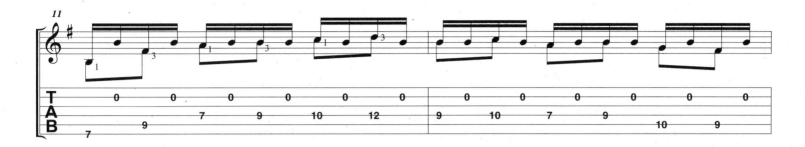

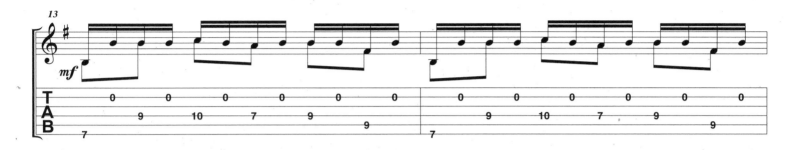

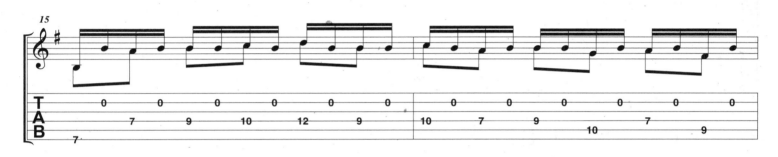

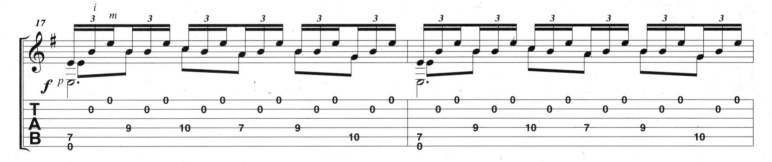

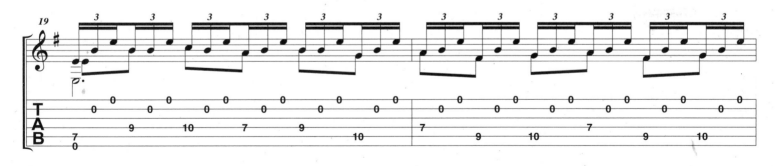

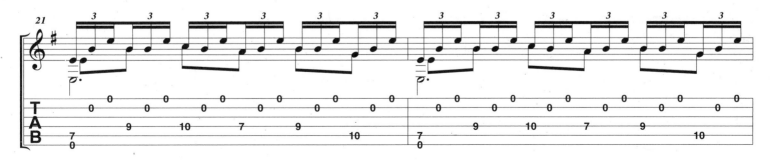

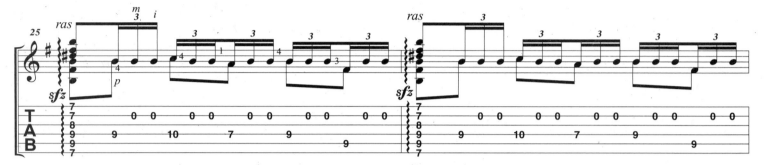

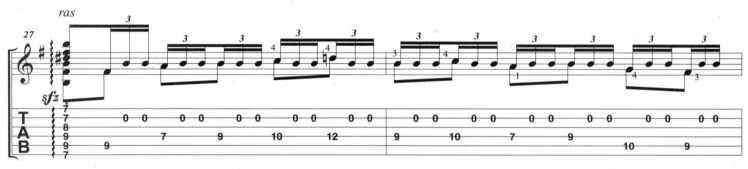

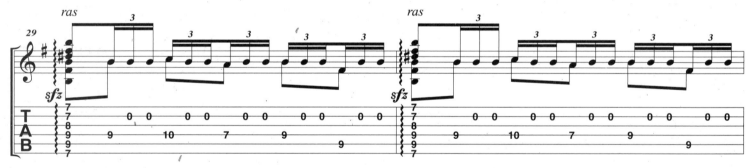

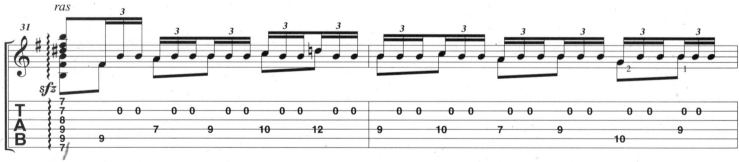

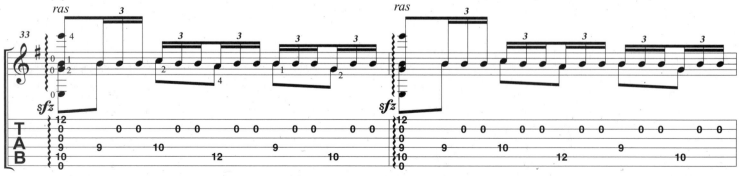

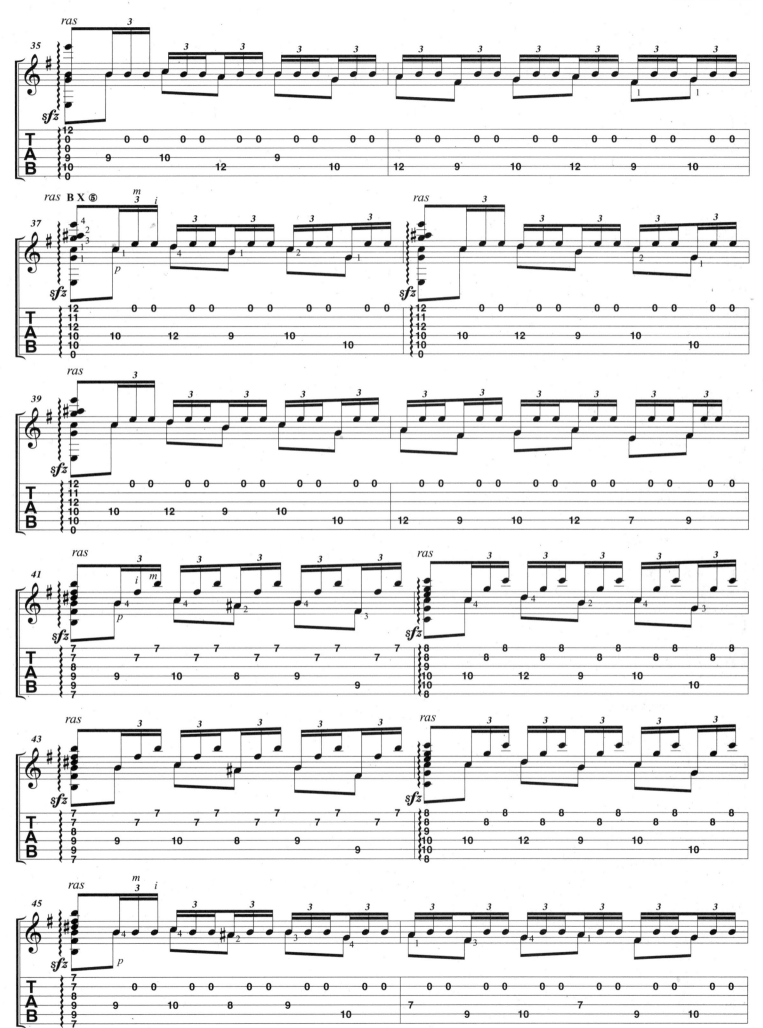

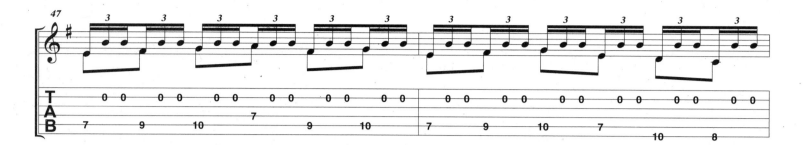

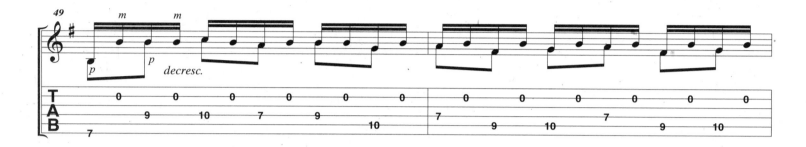

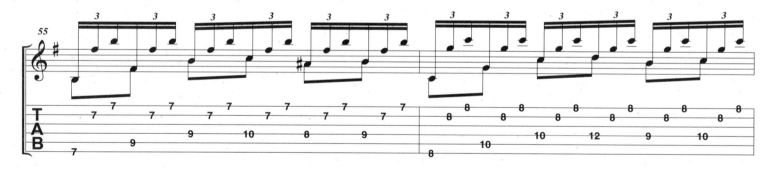

To Coda ⊕

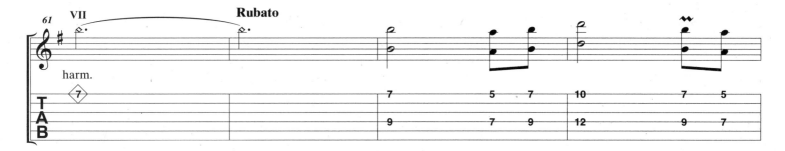

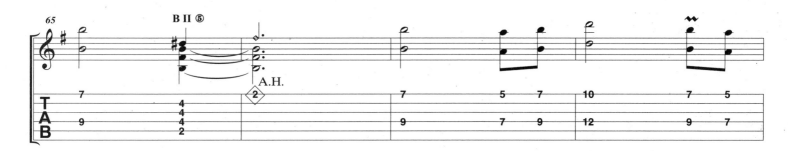

D.C. al Coda

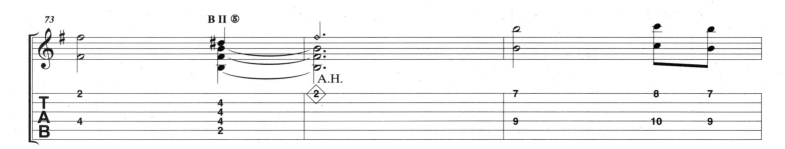

⊕*Coda*

VII Position

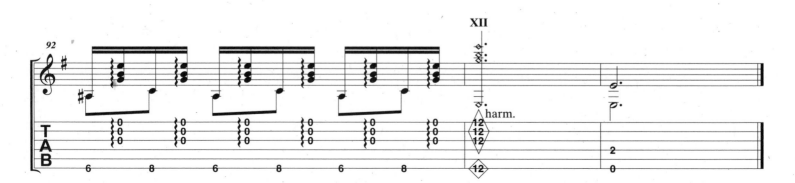

Jesu, Joy of Man's Desiring
Johann Sebastian Bach (1685–1750)

Key Thoughts

"Jesu, Joy of Man's Desiring" was originally the 10th movement from Bach's cantata BWV 147 titled *Herz und Mund und Tat und Leben*, which means "Heart and Mouth and Deed and Life." The word *cantata* literally means "sung," and the work was written for choir with a small orchestra but later transcribed for piano, organ, and guitar in the 20th century. It is probably one of the most popular and requested guitar pieces for weddings and liturgical events.

Take Note

The pulse of this piece clearly lies in the dotted quarter notes that punctuate every beat, but take a larger look at the melodic line. The top line's phrase length could span almost two measures, or as many as four measures, if one so desired. Think and hear the longer line so the piece may flow, and allow the dotted quarter pulse to be nothing more than the gentle heartbeat of the piece. Follow the left- and right-hand fingerings to ensure this piece comes off as a smooth, gently flowing stream of notes and harmony.

TIP

BWV stands for Bach-Werke-Verzeichnis, or "Bach Works Catalogue," which is the numbering system for Bach's works compiled by Wolfgang Schmieder in 1950. The works are not organized chronologically, but rather by category. For example, his lute suites are organized from BWV 995 to 1000, even though they were not written in the same time frame.

GUITAR GODS

JOHANN SEBASTIAN BACH is probably one of the most famous and revered composers in the history of music. Born in Germany, he played the organ, harpsichord, violin, and viola, and his compositions defined the mature baroque period. Though an amazingly prolific writer, he was recognized in his lifetime more as an organist and improviser, and his compositions did not receive wide recognition until the early 19th century thanks to the likes of Mozart, Beethoven, and Chopin. He was a man of strong Lutheran faith, and often signed the scores of his many religious works with *SDG*—"Soli Deo Gloria," meaning "To God Alone Be Glory."

Jesu, Joy of Man's Desiring

Johann Sebastian Bach

Bourrée in E Minor
Johann Sebastian Bach (1685–1750)

Key Thoughts

Probably the oldest of Bach's lute works, the *Lute Suite in E Minor*, BWV 996 was written sometime between 1712 and 1717. This *bourrée* is the fifth movement in this work of six baroque dance forms, preceded by a *praeludio*, *allemande*, *courante*, and *sarabande* and followed by a stunning *giga* that closes the work. Because some of Bach's lute pieces would require using a 14-course lute to effectively play them, it isn't clear if he actually composed them for lute; it is commonly thought they were written for a lute-sounding keyboard called a *lute-harpsichord* or *lautenwerk*, of which Bach owned two. Unfortunately, we will never know, since no examples of this instrument even exist anymore.

Take Note

If there was ever a time to follow fingering, this is it. Left-hand fingers must cover for each other, and it's not always comfortable. The right-hand fingerings must be followed or you will find yourself "painted into a corner" without a finger to save you. Be patient, and it will pay off in the end.

The combination of barres and hinge barres may seem odd at first, but once you get the hang of it, you will understand the reasoning. It's a lot easier to allow underlying strings to ring if you keep the 1st finger extended and hinge it rather than trying to place the tip of the finger on each note indicated with a "1." In these cases, you will hinge from the base of the finger and lift the tip up to allow the lower strings to ring.

FUN FACT

Bach's suites are comprised of multiple movements that are stylized after French court dances of the late 17th and early 18th centuries. The important word here is "stylized," since the intention was never for anyone to dance to them but simply for the music to suggest the spatial feeling of the dance.

GUITAR GODS

Cuban classical guitarist **MANUEL BARRUECO** gives stunning performances of Bach's E major and A minor lute suites on his Vox recording *300 Years of Guitar Masterpieces*. You will find additional Bach works on his EMI Records release *Manuel Barrueco Plays Bach & de Visée*. Visit him at www.barrueco.com.

Bourrée in E Minor

Johann Sebastian Bach

Variations on a Theme by Handel
Mauro Giuliani (1781–1829)

Key Thoughts

A *theme and variation* is a musical form that presents a popular theme and then proceeds to introduce entertaining variations of that theme, creating a whole new work for the listener's pleasure. The theme of this work is based on a melody called "The Harmonious Blacksmith" from George Frideric Handel's *Suite No. 5* for harpsichord. Due to its length, only the theme and two of the variations are presented here, but this work is readily available in numerous classical guitar anthologies if you wish to learn it all.

Take Note

The *hinge barre* introduced in Fernando Sor's "Exercise No. 22" was hinged from the base of the finger, but in this work, the hinge will work from the tip of the finger. Notice in the opening theme how the hinge barre on the 2nd fret goes up and down to minimize finger motion and allow open treble strings to ring underneath. The indicated string number tells you where to place the tip and where it hinges from.

TIP

The fingerings for both left and right hands literally mesh together, with lots of fingers covering for other fingers. As it starts to make sense, write in the other fingerings to make life easier. Be sensitive to this so the correct tempo can be achieved.

GUITAR GODS

MAURO GIULIANI was heralded as the true guitar virtuoso of his time. After leaving his homeland of Italy where guitar opportunities were minimal, he made such a splash in Vienna that, when he later returned to his home country, he was honored with patronage and praise by the Italian nobility. Vienna was the capitol of the European music scene, and Giuliani was the "Guitar Emperor." He was so respected in Vienna that, when Napolean invaded and occupied the territory, he made Giuliani the "virtuoso onorario di camera," or honorary chamber musician, to his second wife, Empress Marie-Louise. (Talk about a tough boss!) Giuliani performed numerous concerts to constant critical acclaim and even gave a duo concert with his guitar virtuoso daughter, Emilia. His influence was so great that after his passing a number of his colleagues published the *Giulianiad,* a periodical that was the predecessor of such publications as *Guitar Player* and *Soundboard* magazines, and contained not only music but also articles and interviews with other famous guitarists.

Variations on a Theme by Handel

Mauro Giuliani

Variation II

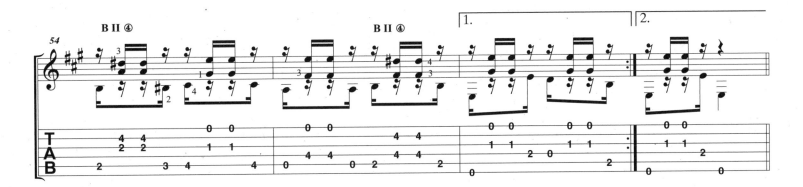

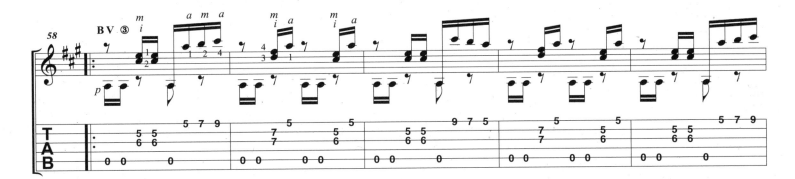

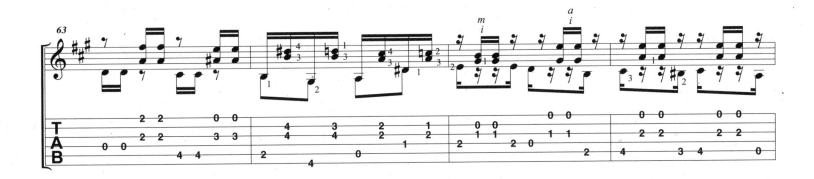

Canon in D
Johann Pachelbel (1653–1706)

Key Thoughts

Pachelbel's "Canon in D" is a work with multiple personalities. In its original orchestration for three violins and *basso continuo*, each violin would play the same melodic line and enter in a staggered fashion two measures apart—hence the title *canon*. But this work also meets the criteria of a *chaconne* in that it has an *ostinato*, or repeating bass line, that allows for variations to occur over the top in the upper voices. Since the solo guitar is unable to truly show the interplay of voices in a canon, then perhaps this work is better described as a chaconne in D when arranged for classical guitar.

Take Note

This arrangement starts with *pizzicatos*, plucked notes that are immediately kept from ringing. To execute a pizzicato, or *pizz*, place the back side of your palm behind the bridge nut to allow the flesh to mute the string. This technique is also called a *palm mute*. Sound the string with the flesh of the thumb as shown.

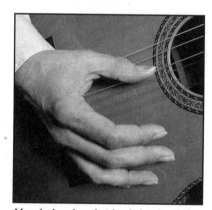

Hand placed on bridge behind saddle.

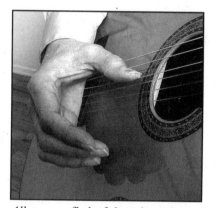

Allow some flesh of the palm to hang over the saddle and mute the strings just a bit so the pitch is still heard.

TIP

Because it is so repetitive, each passage becomes a bit more difficult as you progress. Feel free to repeat the sections that feel comfortable and avoid the ones that don't. Eventually, you will play the entire piece. Be sure to pencil in right-hand fingerings on this one.

FUN FACT

As a highly popular selection, "Canon in D" is one of the most requested works for the processional of a wedding—and rightfully so. One belief is that Pachelbel wrote this canon in October of 1694 for the wedding of Johann Christian Bach, a former pupil and the oldest brother of the future great Johann Sebastian Bach.

Canon in D

Johann Pachelbel
Arranged by Thomas Kikta

Guardame las Vacas
Luis de Narváez (fl. 1526–1549)

Key Thoughts

Throughout musical history, the desire to improvise on a theme has been very strong. Jazz musicians, for example, will present a theme or "head" and then improvise on it to give the piece their own personal touch. You've learned that the *theme and variation* form was very prevalent throughout the classical period, and you also experienced the beauty of baroque *ornamentation* as a way to put a personal touch on a theme. The variations in "Guardame las Vacas" are known as *differencias*, the grand-daddy of all improvisations. This piece is the earliest example of a theme that is then improvised upon to create an exciting example of Renaissance vihuela virtuosity.

Take Note

"Guardame las Vacas" is history's first *romanesca*, a musical form that uses four chords over and over again to create a foundation for improvising a melody. Since it is the earliest example of this form, it is believed to have inspired the romanesca "Greensleeves." Notice the chords that form the foundation in this piece: the progression C, G, Am, and E is played a total of eight times for the purpose of improvisation and then a final ninth time to create the *cadence* that finishes the piece. It will help to memorize it.

The need for fluent *i–m* alternation can't be any more obvious than in this piece. Take a close look at the right-hand fingerings, and work slowly to ensure secure habits that will make this piece sound effortless.

FUN FACT

"Guard My Cows"—that's the direct translation of "Guardame las Vacas." Some believe this was Narváez's tongue-in-cheek comment about some of the more portly members of the royal court, but perhaps he simply wanted his cows watched.

GUITAR GODS

Not much is known about **LUIS DE NARVÁEZ** other than that he was a Spanish composer and vihuelist. The dates of his birth and death are unclear, and the dates fl. 1526–1549 refer to the earliest and latest examples of references to him in documents. A musician in the royal court of the Regent of Spain who later became Spanish King Philip II, in 1538, Narváez published *Los seys libros del Delphín de Música,* a six-volume collection of vihuela music containing fantasias, songs, and most importantly, differencias of which "Guardame las Vacas" is one.

Guardame las Vacas

Luis de Narváez

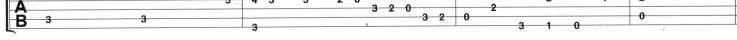

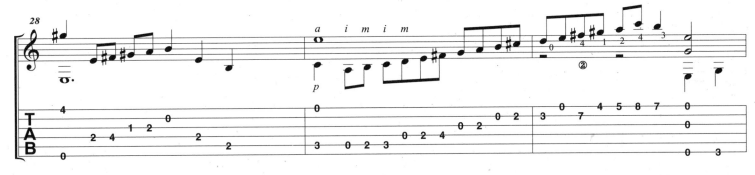

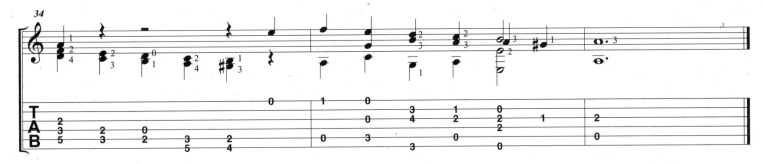

Classical Gas
Mason Williams (b. 1938)

Key Thoughts

"Classical Gas" introduced many people to the beauty and power of pop instrumental guitar music. This piece is another selection that sounds harder than it really is and always tends to wow friends and family. Like many great guitar pieces, it lies very naturally on the instrument. As you go through it, recognize the simple chords that are present.

Take Note

This arrangement is a bit simplified, but pretty close to the original recorded version. The seven-measure intro contains the famous melody, which is played slow and *animato*, meaning without a strong rhythmic pulse.

Playing within the chord shapes is the key to making this flow like the recording, so hold the chord shapes that are created and pick out the correct notes. The ringing will add to the effect.

One of the most identifiable and exciting aspects of this piece is that it has many interesting rhythmic changes. For example, notice the $\frac{6}{4}$ time signature in measure 28, where the series of arpeggios creates an interesting tension by accenting groups of three notes instead of groups of two. It's easy to play—just identify the chord and arpeggiate away with a constant stream of eighth notes. Go through and identify the numerous arpeggios used in this piece.

In measure 12, a percussive effect called a *golpe* is performed. To do this, just thump the thumb on the face of the guitar as shown here.

Tap the face of the guitar with the thumb to perform a golpe.

Spirited ♩ = 169

GUITAR GODS

MASON WILLIAMS was already an Emmy Award-winning comedy writer for the *Smothers Brothers Comedy Hour* when he broke out as a virtuoso guitar artist in the 1960s. Warner Bros. Records was looking to add 10 new artists at the time, and Tom Smothers suggested the label give Williams a chance. In 1968, he released his first effort, *The Mason Williams Phonograph Record*, which peaked at No. 14 and won two Grammy Awards for the chart-topping hit "Classical Gas."

Classical Gas

Mason Williams

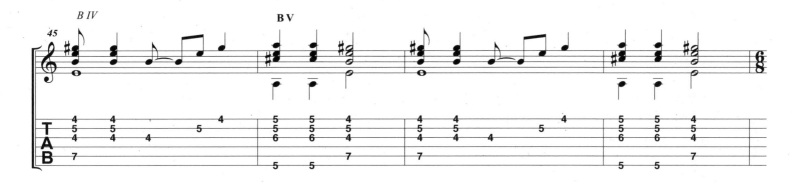

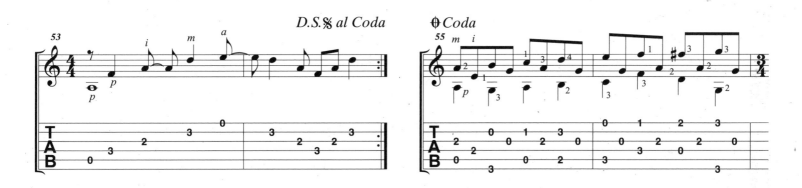

D.S. 𝄋 *al Coda*

𝄌 *Coda*

Ashokan Farewell
Jay Ungar (b. 1946)

In 1982, after closing his summer string festival in Ashokan, New York, Jay Ungar was feeling pretty blue over the fact that a beautiful experience had ended and he had to return to the hassles of everyday life. Out of that emotion came this lament, "Ashokan Farewell," and when PBS producer Ken Burns heard it, he made it the theme to his 1990 television miniseries, *The Civil War*.

In most classical guitar pieces, when it comes to right-hand fingering, generally the thumb takes the bass and the fingers take the melody, creating two different sounds that keep those voices distinct. This is not the case here. Instead, the melody is voiced low so that a dark, haunting growl comes out of the guitar, and with that comes the problem of *cross voicings*. The key is to emphasize the melody no matter where it goes or what finger or thumb must play it. Then, all other notes, regardless of register, are accompaniment and should be kept in the background. This creates the illusion of two guitars in ensemble.

DEFINITION

A **cross voicing** occurs when a melody crosses lower than its accompaniment. This can sound very odd unless you give proper emphasis to the melody.

There are two options for the repeat of the main theme that occurs at measure 32. The easy option is to play it an octave higher than shown, but a beautiful alternative is to play the melody with artificial harmonics using *i* to stop the string for the harmonic while *a* sounds it. This leaves *p* and *m* free to play natural notes and create a compelling contrast. This technique is illustrated in the lesson for "El Noi de la Mare." As the left hand moves with the melody, so must the right, always maintaining a 12-fret distance.

The following shows the same passage but without the artificial harmonics.

Alternate measures 32–40 (Without harmonics)

Ashokan Farewell

Jay Ungar
Arranged by Thomas Kikta

⑥ = D

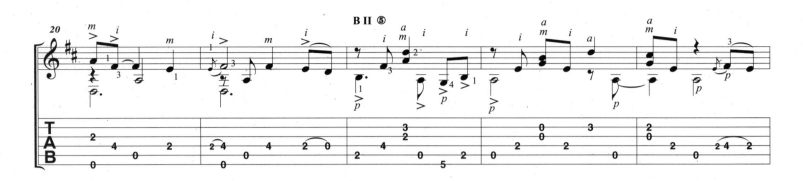

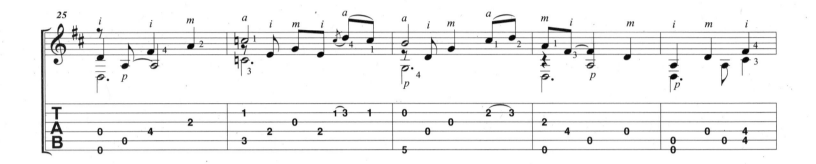

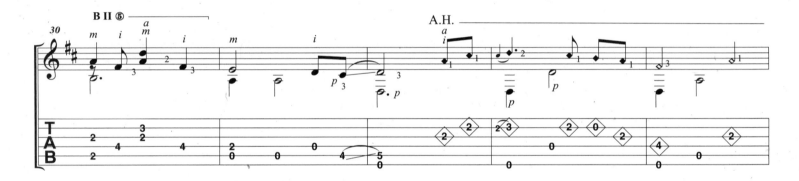

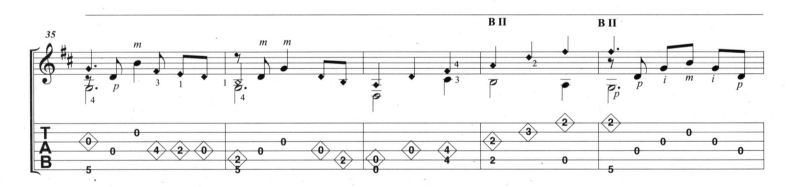

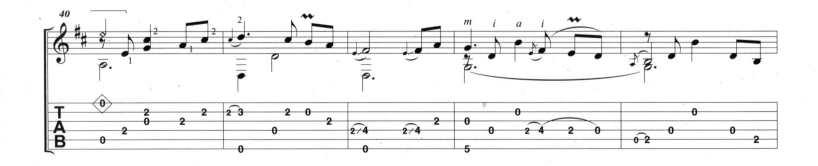

Simple Gifts
Elder Joseph Brackett (1797–1882)

Key Thoughts

When Elder Joseph Bracket wrote "Simple Gifts" in 1848, his intention was for it to be a simple dance song to be performed in his Shaker community. Little did he know it would go down through the ages as an anthem for Americana. This arrangement explores the *altered tuning* DADGAD and demonstrates how the classical technique you have acquired can also be used effectively on steel strings—nails and all.

Take Note

To tune your guitar to DADGAD, maintain the standard tuning of the 5th, 4th, and 3rd strings and lower the 6th, 2nd, and 1st strings one whole step. Notice that the resulting open string tuning forms a D suspended 4th chord. This gives DADGAD a uniquely ambiguous harmonic quality—neither inherently major nor minor— that makes it especially useful for drone-like harmonies as in the beginning of "Simple Gifts," or Celtic music where the harmony often begins as an ambiguous drone and builds in complexity with each repetition.

TIP

Since the guitar is now rather radically tuned from how you're accustomed, it might be beneficial to rely a bit more on the TAB rather than relearning the instrument. Doing so can also be helpful in the future when learning selections that are far more "altered" in tuning than this one.

Primarily, the piece is composed of an open-string drone with the melody laid out on top. You can just play the melody over the top of the dulcimer-like drone, but remember to play the proper bass note D or A at the correct time.

GUITAR GODS

One day at Peabody Conservatory in the early 1980s, Aaron Shearer told **MICHAEL HEDGES** in his last guitar lesson, "Hmmmmm… son, you will never be a classic guitarist," and Shearer was so right! Hedges went on to redefine the guitar as we knew it, combining new ways of tapping, beating, and cajoling amazing melodies out of it. A composition major, he morphed the guitar to the music he heard in his head, creating altered tunings that supported his genius. Be sure to discover the treasures he gave us, for he was with us far too briefly— tragically, he lost his life in a car accident in December of 1997.

If you want to take it to the next level, some tapping, harmonic slaps, and beats played with the palm, knuckle, and thumb have been incorporated to make things more interesting. This simple piece is perfect for practicing these techniques and learning how to weave them in. The following is a key for the symbols. Take note that these are not standard symbols; composers tend to use various symbols and provide a legend such as this one.

Palm hit on guitar face

Knuckle hit on guitar face

Thumb hit on guitar face

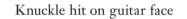

Nails hit on guitar face

Harmonic slap

To play a *harmonic slap*, whip the right-hand index finger with a quick wrist action so that it impacts at the indicated fret.

Simple Gifts

Elder Joseph Brackett
Arranged by Thomas Kikta

Gtr. tuned to DADGAD:
⑥ = D   ③ = G
⑤ = A   ② = A
④ = D   ① = D

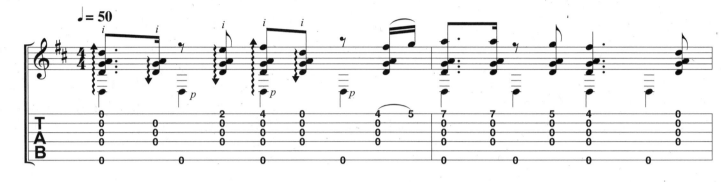

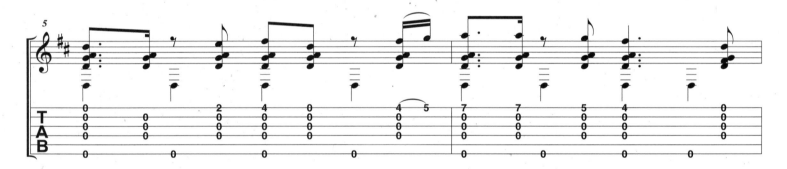

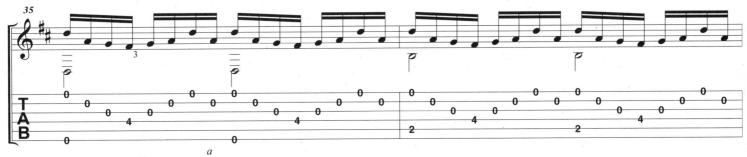

Music Theory 1-2-3

You don't have to understand music theory to play the selections in this book. The music notation, TAB, and fingerings tell you everything you need to know to play the music correctly. But to gain a greater appreciation of the music and, someday, be able to make good musical decisions on your own with little information, you will want to know the theory. This section will help you get a footing towards understanding music theory and organization. I call it "Music Theory 1–2–3" because we are going to start with the single-note organization of scales, then proceed to two-note combinations of intervals, and end up with three or more notes forming chords.

Scales

A *scale* is a series of notes organized in a specific pattern of *whole steps* and *half steps*. To explore this, play a note on the guitar and then play the next note one fret above it; this is the distance of a half step. If you play two frets above a note, the distance is a whole step.

The *major* scale is the most commonly used scale. The pattern of the major scale is two whole steps, then a half step, followed by three whole steps, and finishing with a final half step (1–1–½–1–1–1–½), as shown below. Notice the half steps between the 3rd and 4th notes and the 7th and 8th notes. Changing the order of half steps and whole steps would create a scale with a very different sound. The first note of a scale is called the *tonic*.

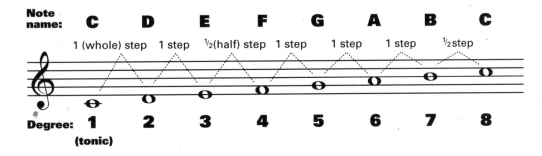

Key Signatures

In music, *key signatures* show all the sharps and flats necessary to maintain the arrangement of whole and half steps in the corresponding scale. Below, the *circle of fifths* shows all the major scales and their associated key signatures. The circle of fifths provides a quick reference to the relationship of the keys and how key signatures can be figured out in a logical manner. Moving clockwise provides all of the sharp keys by progressively adding one sharp to the key signature. Moving counter-clockwise provides the flat keys by progressively adding one flat to the key signature.

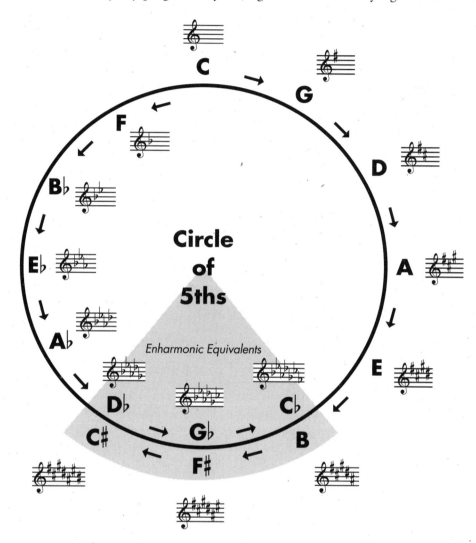

Major and Minor

For every major key signature, there is a corresponding *minor* key. The notes of a minor scale can be found by starting on the 6th note of a major scale. For example, the C major scale is played C–D–E–F–G–A–B–C, with the half steps between the 3rd and 4th notes and the 7th and 8th notes. Playing the same notes from A to A creates the minor scale, which has a different, darker sound than the major scale.

In a minor scale, the order of whole steps and half steps is different than the major scale, which gives it a different quality. The half steps are now between the 2nd and 3rd notes and the 6th and 7th notes. This creates a dark and melancholy sound.

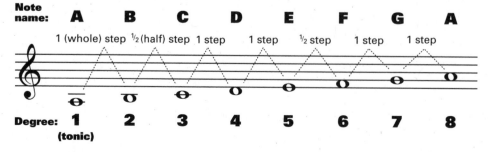

Scales that share the same key signature are known as *relative major* and *relative minor*. For example, the relative minor of C major is A minor, and the relative major of A minor is C major. The key signature for both contains no sharps or flats, which is equivalent to playing just the white keys of a piano. To quickly figure out a major key's relative minor, just count up to the 6th note of the major scale.

Major Key	Relative Minor
C	A
G	E
D	B
A	F♯
E	C♯
B (C♭)	G♯ (A♭)
F♯ (G♭)	D♯ (E♭)
C♯ (D♭)	A♯ (B♭)
A♭	F
E♭	C
B♭	G
F	D

For the record, there are three different flavors of minor scales. The one that you just learned is called the *natural minor*, and the notes are identical to the notes of the major scale but starting on the 6th degree.

The *harmonic minor* scale is the natural minor with the 7th degree raised a half step.

The *melodic minor* has the 6th and 7th degrees raised a half step when a melodic line is ascending and lowered back to normal when descending. Bach's "Bourrée in E Minor" on page 109 of this book uses the E melodic minor scale.

A Natural Minor

A Harmonic Minor

A Melodic Minor

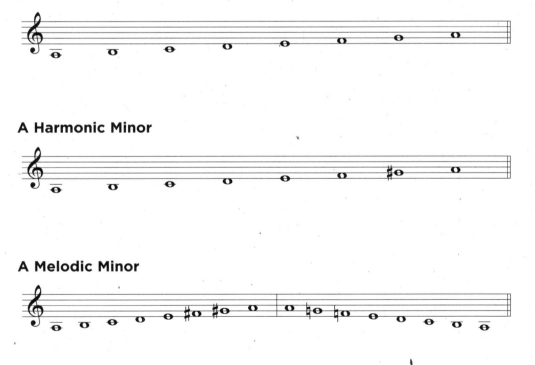

Intervals

Okay, this is the meat of the matter, so pay attention: An *interval* is the distance between two notes. We need to learn a few things about how to define that distance.

There are two parts to defining an interval: the name of the interval (2nd, 3rd, 4th, 5th, and so on) and the *quality* of the interval. Below is our friendly C major scale again with the *scale degrees* (numbers) labeled as well as the intervals.

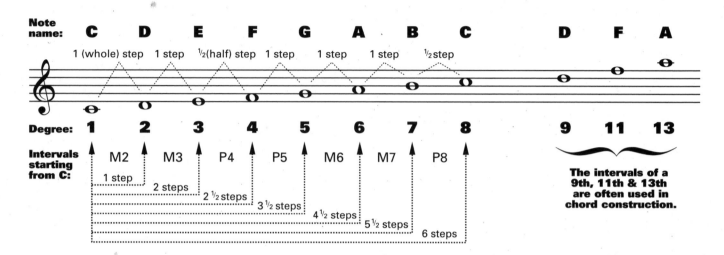

The name of an interval is determined by counting the number of scale degrees from one note to the next. For example, an interval of a 3rd up from C is determined by counting up three scale degrees: C–D–E (1–2–3). C to E is a 3rd. A 4th from C is determined by counting up four scale degrees: C–D–E–F (1–2–3–4). C to F is a 4th.

In addition to the name that defines the distance between scale degrees, every interval has a *quality*. An interval's quality is determined by counting the number of whole steps and half steps between the two notes. For example, C to E is a 3rd, but it is also a *major* 3rd because there are two whole steps (four half steps) between them. Likewise, C to E♭ is a 3rd, but it is a *minor* 3rd because there are only one and a half steps (three half steps) between them.

There are five qualities used to describe intervals: *major, minor, perfect, diminished,* and *augmented*. When stating an interval, you will always give a quality and a number.

Quality	Abbreviation
major	M
minor	m
perfect	P
diminished	dim or °
augmented	aug or +

Particular intervals are associated with certain qualities. Not all qualities pertain to every type of interval, as seen in the following table.

Interval Type	Possible Qualities
2nd, 9th	major, minor, augmented
3rd, 6th, 13th	major, minor, diminished, augmented
4th, 5th, 11th	perfect, diminished, augmented
7th	major, minor, diminished

Ok what does this all mean? We now have a language by which we can communicate the distances between notes. Let's learn a little system to make it easy to identify intervals. Here is an interval with C on the bottom and E on the top.

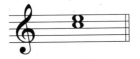

1. The bottom note tells you what key you're going to use to figure out the interval. In this case, the note is C, so the key is C major.

2. Counting C as 1, count from C to E: C–D–E, so 1–2–3. Okay—it's a 3rd of some sort.

3. Now, ask yourself: Is E a member of the C major scale? YES. It is therefore a *major 3rd*.

   The quality of intervals are as follows when the top note is a member of the bottom note's major scale:

   2nd, 3rd, 6th, 7th = major

   1st (unison), 4th, 5th, 8th (octave) = perfect

   When the top note of an interval is not a member of the bottom note's scale, such as E♭ above C, you must ask a fourth question:

4. How was the top note altered such that it is not a member of the scale?

Whenever a major interval is lowered by a half step, it becomes a *minor* interval. In this case, the E was lowered a half step to E♭, which defines it as a *minor third*.

The following table shows how the other qualities are affected by lowering or raising an interval by a half step.

Quality	Alteration	Result
major	lowered a half step	minor
major	raised a half step	augmented
minor	lowered a half step	diminished
perfect	lowered a half step	diminished
perfect	raised a half step	augmented

Check out these examples and use the steps to confirm the answers.

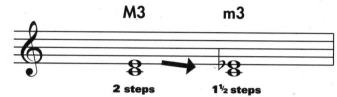

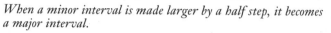

When a major interval is made smaller by a half step, it becomes a minor interval.

When a minor interval is made larger by a half step, it becomes a major interval.

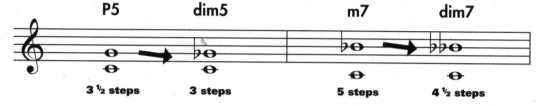

When a perfect or minor interval is made smaller by a half step, it becomes a diminished interval.

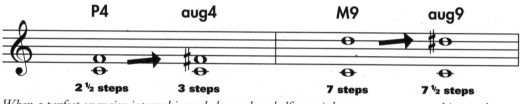

When a perfect or major interval is made larger by a half step, it becomes an augmented interval.

The following table of intervals uses C as the bottom note. Notice that some intervals are labeled *enharmonic*, which means that they are written differently but sound the same.

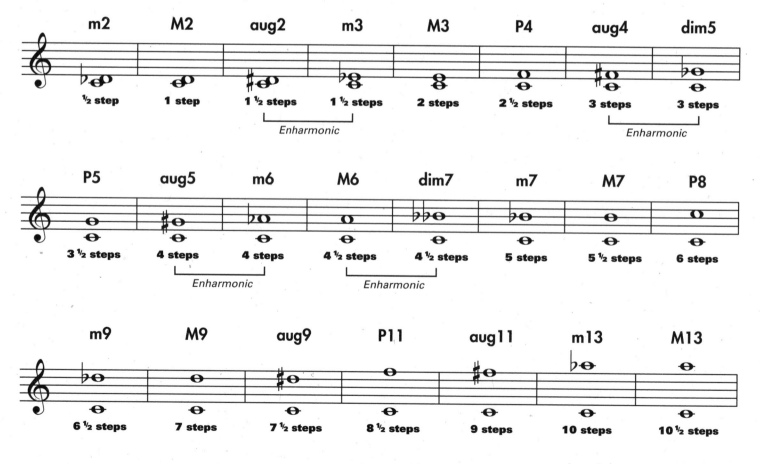

Basic Triads

Chords are intervals that are combined together. For example, a *major chord* is created from the 1st, 3rd, and 5th degrees of a major scale; the intervals from the tonic are a major 3rd and a perfect 5th. C–E–G is a C major chord, G–B–D is a G major chord, and so on. A three-note chord is called a *triad*, and there are four types: major, minor, diminished, and augmented.

Try it on your guitar: Play an old cowboy C chord in 1st position. Notice that the notes are a combination of C, E, and G. Pretty cool!

The following table shows how notes are altered to create chords with different qualities. As an exercise, explore all the chords you know to discover why they are major, minor, diminished, or augmented.

Scale Degrees	Chord Quality
1–3–5	major
1–♭3–5	minor
1–♭3–♭5	diminished
1–3–♯5	augmented

Chord Inversions

When speaking about chords, the 1st degree of the scale, such as the C in a C chord, is the *root*. A chord with the root at the bottom is in *root position*. It's important to know that chords can be *inverted* so that the root is not played as the bottom note. If the root of a triad is moved above the 5th so that the 3rd is the bottom note of the chord, it is said to be in *first inversion*. If the root and 3rd are moved above the 5th, making the 5th the bottom note, then the chord is in *second inversion*.

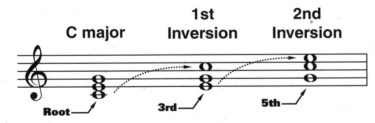

Building Chords

By using the four chord types as basic building blocks, it is possible to create a variety of chords by adding 6ths, 7ths, 9ths, 11ths, and so on. The following are examples of some of the many variations.

C Major Suspended Fourth
Csus

C Diminished
C°

C Major Add Ninth
C(add9)
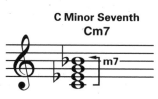

C Diminished 7th
C°7

C Major Sixth
C6
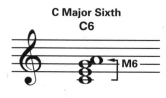

C Sixth Add Ninth
C6/9
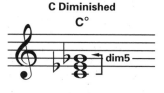

C Minor Sixth Add Ninth
Cm6/9
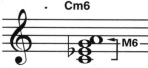

C Minor Sixth
Cm6

C Dominant Seventh
C7
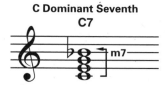

C Seventh Suspended Fourth
C7sus

C Minor Seventh
Cm7
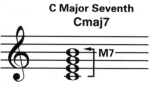

C Minor Seventh Flat Fifth
Cm7(♭5)

C Seventh Augmented Fifth
C7+
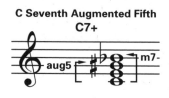

C Seventh Flat Fifth
C7(♭5)
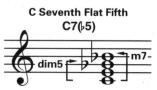

C Major Seventh
Cmaj7
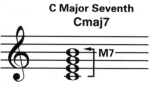

C Major Seventh Flat Fifth
Cmaj7(♭5)
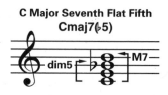

C Minor Major Seventh
Cm(maj7)
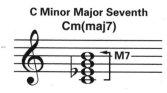

C Seventh Flat Ninth
C7(♭9)
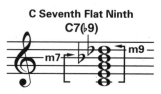

C Seventh Augmented Ninth
C7(♯9)
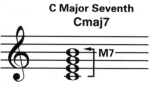

C Seventh Flat Ninth Augmented Fifth
C7+(♭9)
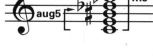

C Minor Ninth
Cm9
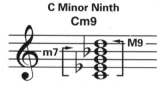

C Ninth
C9
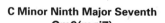

C Ninth Augmented Fifth
C9+
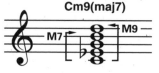

C Ninth Flat Fifth
C9(♭5)
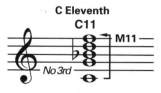

C Major Ninth
Cmaj9
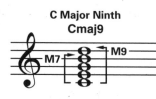

C Ninth Augmented Eleventh
C9(♯11)
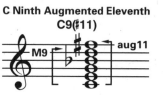

C Minor Ninth Major Seventh
Cm9(maj7)
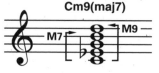

C Eleventh
C11
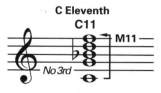

C Minor Eleventh
Cm11
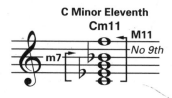

C Thirteenth
C13
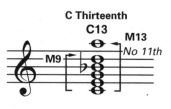

C Thirteenth Flat Ninth
C13(♭9)
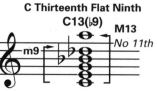

C Thirteenth Flat Ninth Flat Fifth
C13(♭9♭5)
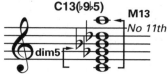

So far, the examples provided to illustrate intervals and chord construction have been based on C. Until you're familiar with chords, the C chord examples on the previous page can serve as a guide for building chords based on other notes. For example, to construct a G7(♭9) chord, you can first determine what intervals are contained in C7(♭9) and use the steps below to build the same chord starting on G.

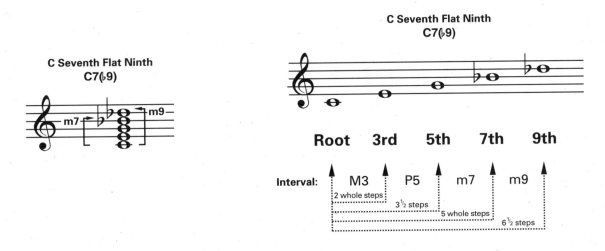

- First, determine the *root* of the chord. A chord is always named for its root, so G is the root of G7(♭9).

- Count *letter names* up from the *letter name of the root* (G) to determine the intervals of the chord. Counting three letter names up from G to B (G–A–B, 1–2–3) is a 3rd, G to D (G–A–B–C–D) is a 5th, G to F is a 7th, and G to A is a 9th.

- Determine the *quality* of the intervals by counting half steps and whole steps up from the root. G to B (2 whole steps) is a major 3rd, G to D (3½ steps) is a perfect 5th, G to F (5 whole steps) is a minor 7th, and G to A♭ (6½ steps) is a minor 9th.

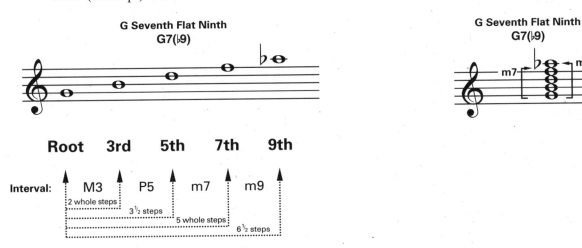

Follow this general guideline for determining the notes of any chord. As intervals and chord construction become more familiar to you, you'll be able to create original fingerings on the guitar. Don't be afraid to experiment!

Guitar
Fingerboard Chart

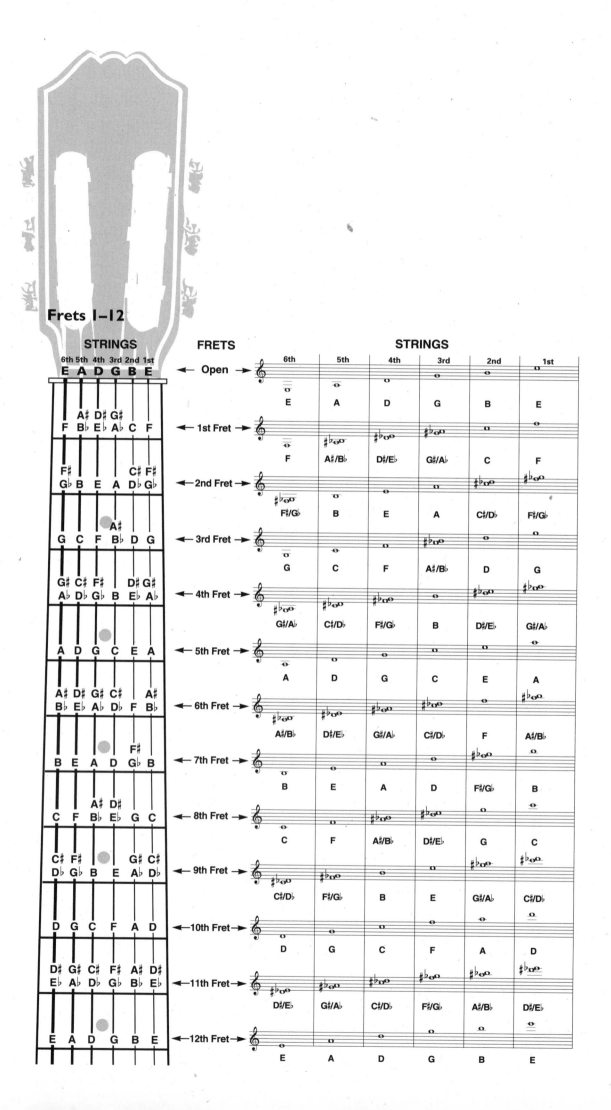

Frets 1–12

Suggested Reading and Listening

Guitar Methods by Aaron Shearer

Classic Guitar Technique, Volume 1

Classic Guitar Technique, Volume 2

Classic Guitar Technique, Supplement 1: Slur, Ornament, and Reach Development Exercises

Classic Guitar Technique, Supplement 2: Basic Elements of Music Theory for the Guitar

Classic Guitar Technique, Supplement 3: Scale Pattern Studies for Guitar

Learning the Classic Guitar, Part 1

Learning the Classic Guitar, Part 2

Learning the Classic Guitar, Part 3

About the Instrument

The Art and Craft of Making Classical Guitars by Manuel Rodriguez

The Classical Guitar Book: A Complete History by Balafon Books

The Complete Encyclopedia of the Guitar by Terry Burrows

Guitars by Tom and Mary Anne Evans

Suggested Guitar Organizations

Guitar Foundation of America www.guitarfoundation.org

The Aaron Shearer Foundation www.aaronshearerfoundation.org

Classical/Crossover Guitar Recording Artists

Muriel Anderson

Assad Brothers (Odair and Sergio Assad)

Beijing Guitar Duo (Meng Su and Yameng Wang)

Carlos Barbosa-Lima

Agustín Barrios Mangoré

Manuel Barrueco

Pierre Bensusan

Julian Bream

Ricardo Cobo

Roland Dyens

Eduardo Fernández

Michael Hedges

Adam Holzman

Sharon Isbin

William Kanengiser

Adrian Legg

Los Angeles Guitar Quartet

Christopher Parkening

The Romeros (including Angel and Pepe Romero)

Andrés Segovia

Raphaella Smits

David Starobin

David Tanenbaum

Scott Tennant

Ralph Towner

Benjamin Verdery

Anne Vidovic

Jason Vieaux

John Williams

Andrew York

Music History Timeline

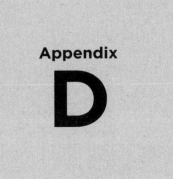

HISTORICAL EVENTS

**PRINTING PRESS
INVENTED (1440)**

**COLUMBUS ARRIVES
IN AMERICA**

Historical Figures

Leonardo da Vinci 1452-1519

Galileo Galilei

Michelangelo 1475-1564

Christopher Columbus 1451-1506

William Shake

1450	1460	1470	1480	1490	1500	1510	1520	1530	1540	1550	1560	1570

Musical Periods

Renaissance Era

Composers, Teachers,
and Performers of Music
for Fretted Instruments

John Dowland

Luys Milán 1500-1561

Vincenzo Galilei c. 1520-1591

Luis de Narváez fl. 1526-1549

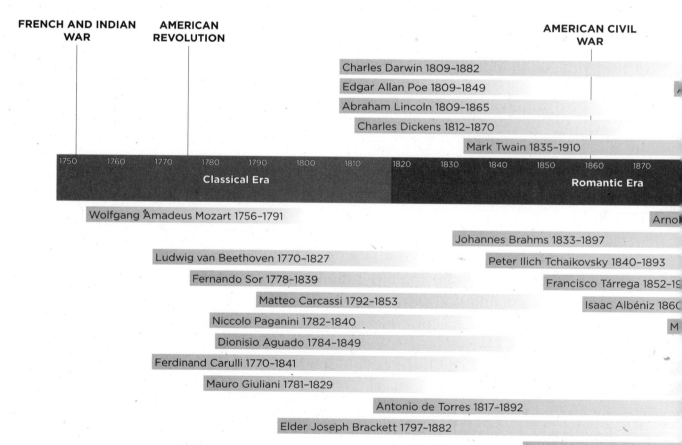

**FRENCH AND INDIAN
WAR**

**AMERICAN
REVOLUTION**

**AMERICAN CIVIL
WAR**

Charles Darwin 1809-1882

Edgar Allan Poe 1809-1849

Abraham Lincoln 1809-1865

Charles Dickens 1812-1870

Mark Twain 1835-1910

1750	1760	1770	1780	1790	1800	1810	1820	1830	1840	1850	1860	1870

Classical Era

Romantic Era

Wolfgang Amadeus Mozart 1756-1791

Arno

Johannes Brahms 1833-1897

Ludwig van Beethoven 1770-1827

Peter Ilich Tchaikovsky 1840-1893

Fernando Sor 1778-1839

Francisco Tárrega 1852-19

Matteo Carcassi 1792-1853

Isaac Albéniz 1860

Niccolo Paganini 1782-1840

M

Dionisio Aguado 1784-1849

Ferdinand Carulli 1770-1841

Mauro Giuliani 1781-1829

Antonio de Torres 1817-1892

Elder Joseph Brackett 1797-1882

Oscar Chilesotti 1848-1916

JAMESTOWN   PILGRIMS SAIL
SETTLED   THE MAYFLOWER

42

Rembrandt 1609-1669

George Washington
1732-1799

564-1616

Ben Franklin 1706-1790

| 1590 | 1600 | 1610 | 1620 | 1630 | 1640 | 1650 | 1660 | 1670 | 1680 | 1690 | 1700 | 1710 | 1720 | 1730 | 1740 | 1750 |

Baroque Era

Johann Pachelbel 1653-1706

Franz Joseph Haydn
1732-1809

Henry Purcell 1659-1695

Christian Petzold 1677-1733

Domenico Scarlatti 1685-1757

George Frideric Handel 1685-1759

Johann Sebastian Bach 1685-1750

Sylvius Leopold Weiss 1686-1750

26

Antonio Vivaldi 1678-1741

Gaspar Sanz 1640-1710

Johann Philipp Krieger 1649-1725

Robert de Visée 1650-1725

WRIGHT   WORLD WAR   WORLD WAR   WOODSTOCK
BROTHERS FLY   I   II

instein 1879-1955

George Balanchine 1904-1983

Andy Warhol 1928-1987

| 1890 | 1900 | 1910 | 1920 | 1930 | 1940 | 1950 | 1960 | 1970 | 1980 | 1990 | 2000 | 2010 |

Modern/Contemporary Era

enberg 1874-1951

Jay Ungar b. 1946

Aaron Copland 1900-1990

Leonard Bernstein 1918-1990

Mason Williams b. 1938

obet 1878-1938

Andrés Segovia 1893-1987

ustín Barrios Mangoré 1885-1944

Heitor Villa-Lobos 1887-1959

Aaron Shearer 1919-2008

Leo Brouwer b. 1939

Common Italian Music Terms

Tempo

largo	extremely slow
lento	very slow
adagio	slow
andante	moderately slow
moderato	moderate speed
allegretto	somewhat fast
allegro	fast
vivace	lively
presto	very fast
prestissimo	extremely fast
accelerando (accel.)	gradually becoming faster
ritardando (rit.)	gradually becoming slower
a tempo	return to original tempo
animato	animated
con moto	with motion
meno mosso	with less motion; less quickly
rubato	with expressive tempo changes
fermata ⌒	pause

Form Indications

da capo (D.C.)	the beginning
dal segno (D.S.)	the sign 𝄋
fine	the end
coda	the tail, final section of a piece

Dynamics

fortissimo (ff)		very loud
forte (f)		loud
mezzo forte (mf)		moderately loud
mezzo piano (mp)		moderately soft
piano (p)		soft
pianissimo (pp)		very soft
crescendo (cresc.)	⟍	gradually getting louder
decrescendo (decresc.)	⟋	gradually getting softer
diminuendo (dim.)	⟍	gradually getting softer
sforzando (sf)		a strong accent on a single note
sforzato (sfz)		a strong accent on a single note

Terms for Musical Expression

agitato	agitated
brio	brilliance
cantabile	in a singing style
dolce	sweet
energico	energetic
espressivo	expressive
grandioso	grand
grazioso	graceful

legato	smooth
maestoso	majestic
marcato	with emphasis
risoluto	resolute
scherzando	playful
sostenuto	sustained
staccato	detached, choppy

Other Terms

con	with
meno	less
molto	much
piu	more
poco	little
poco a poco	little by little
primo	first
quasi	almost
secondo	second
sempre	always
senza	without
simile	in a similar manner
troppo / non troppo	too much / not too much

Examples

con brio	with brilliance
allegro quasi presto	allegro, almost presto
sempre cantabile	always in a singing style
molto espressivo	with much expression
senza ritardando	without slowing down

Glossary

accent Emphasis on a beat, note, or chord.

acciaccatura Meaning "to crush," a quick ornamental note played on the beat just before the main note. Play this ornamental note as if it is hot to the touch.

accidental A sharp, flat, or natural sign that occurs in a measure, altering the note from the key.

allemande A 17th-century stylized dance type, often used for the first movement of a baroque suite following the prelude.

altered tuning Any tuning other than standard tuning on the guitar.

alternation A right-hand movement in which two fingers trade off to sound the strings; as one finger plays, the other prepares.

animato To play a musical passage in an animated fashion, with lots of feeling and without regard to meter.

appoggiatura Meaning "to lean upon," a decorative note that displaces and then resolves to the main note.

arpeggio The notes of a chord played one after another instead of simultaneously. For classical guitarists, this also refers to right-hand patterns that are played while holding a chord, such as *p–i–m–a* or *p–a–m–i*.

arpeggios without *p* Five arpeggios that do not use the thumb: *a–i–m*, *a–m–i–m*, *a–i–m–i*, *a–m–i*, and *i–a–m–a*.

artificial harmonic A bell-like sound produced by fretting with the left hand, touching harmonic points with the right-hand index finger, then plucking the string with *a*. Complete melodies can be played this way even with natural bass counterpoint.

bar See *measure*.

bar line A vertical line that indicates where one measure ends and another begins.

baroque period Music historians have given this title to the years 1600 to 1750, approximately. See Appendix D.

baroque tablature Notation systems used by lute and vihuela players, similar to today's system.

barre To fret multiple strings with one finger.

barre chord A chord played by fretting several strings with one finger.

basso continuo Any instrument or instruments that would provide the foundation of a baroque work, including the harpsichord, guitar, lute, organ, or harp, since these instruments can provide harmony with bass.

bourrée A light, rapid dance form often used in 17th-century baroque suites.

bridge The part of the guitar that anchors the strings to the body.

cadence A chord progression that brings a section to a close.

canon A type of polyphony in which a theme is stated in one voice and then strictly repeated in others.

cantata A baroque, multi-movement vocal work.

capo A device placed around the neck of a guitar to raise the pitch of the strings.

chaconne A baroque form in which variations are continuously created over a repeating bass line.

chamber music   Classical music written for small ensemble so that it could be played in royal chambers.

chord   A group of three or more notes played simultaneously.

chord progression   A sequence of chords played in succession.

classical period   Music historians have given this title to the years 1750 to 1820, approximately. See Appendix D.

common time   The most prevalent time signature in music. In common time, there are four beats to every measure and the quarter note gets one beat. Same as $\frac{4}{4}$.

comping   A slang term for accompanying someone with a musical instrument.

contemporary period   Music historians have given this title to the period beginning in 1910 to the present, approximately. See Appendix D.

countermelody   A melody played at the same time as the main melody.

counterpoint   The relationship between two or more independent voices in music.

courante   A 17th-century stylized dance type, often used for the second movement after the prelude of a baroque suite.

course   Paired strings on a fretted instrument tuned in octaves or unisons, similar to those of a modern-day 12-string guitar.

cross fingering   A situation that occurs in the right hand when a lower finger must reach for a higher string while a higher finger reaches for a lower string, such as *i* playing the open B string while *m* plays the open G string. The fingers literally cross.

cross voicing   When a higher voice goes below a lower voice in counterpoint.

cut time   A time signature that usually indicates a faster tempo. In cut time, there are two beats to every measure and the half note gets one beat. Same as $\frac{2}{2}$.

DADGAD tuning   A guitar tuning in which the 6th, 2nd, and 1st strings are tuned down a whole step.

differencias   An early form of variation in which a theme is first stated and then varied upon each repetition. "Guardame las Vacas" is the earliest known example of this form.

dotted note   A note followed by a dot, indicating that the length of the note is longer by one half of the note's original length.

double bar line   A sign made of one thin line and one thick line, indicating the end of a piece of music.

double stop   A group of two notes played simultaneously.

downbeat   The first beat of a measure.

drop D tuning   An altered tuning in which the 6th string of the guitar is lowered from E to D.

dulcimer   An Appalachian fretted instrument having a melody string along with drone strings that are tuned in octaves and fifths.

eighth note   A note equal to half a quarter note, or one half beat in $\frac{4}{4}$ time.

eighth rest   A rest equal to the duration of an eighth note.

etude   A composition that focuses on a particular technical skill. In French, the word means "study."

extension   To extend the fingers, such as opening your fingers from a fist. This is the opposite of *flexion*.

fantasia   A musical form that encourages "freedom" and "flight of fancy" over strict formal structure.

fermata   A symbol that indicates to hold a note for about twice as long as usual.

fifth   The fifth note of a scale above the root note, the distance of seven half steps.

fingerboard   See *fretboard*.

fingerpicking   A style of playing that uses the right hand fingers to pluck the guitar strings rather than using a pick.

fingerstyle   See *fingerpicking*.

flamenco guitar   A style of guitar and guitar playing that finds its roots in the Andalusian region of Spain. This Spanish folk music style is generally accompanied with folk dancing.

flat   A symbol that indicates to lower a note one half step.

flexion   To close the fingers, such as closing the fingers into a fist. This is the opposite of *extension*.

follow-through   A technique that allows the right-hand finger to continue moving unimpeded after it sounds a string. The fingers follow through toward the palm, which allows the natural timing of flexion and extension to occur.

free stroke   A right-hand finger stroke that allows the finger to pass freely over the next adjacent string after sounding a string.

fretboard   The part of the guitar neck where the frets lay.

frets   The metal strips across the fretboard of a guitar.

G clef   See *treble clef.*

giga   A lively dance form, often used for a quick closing movement in a baroque suite.

glide or guide finger   A finger left on the fingerboard to guide the hand to a new movement. Can be performed with or without a glissando.

glissando (gliss.)   A melodic connection of two notes. One note will slide melodically to the next.

golpe   A percussive effect performed by tapping on the guitar with the thumb or fingers.

half note   A note equal to two quarter notes, or two beats in $\frac{4}{4}$ time.

half rest   A rest equal to the duration of a half note.

half step   The distance of one fret on the guitar.

hammer-on   A technique by which a note is made to sound after playing the string with the right hand by tapping down on the string with another finger of the fretting hand.

harmonic slap   To whip or slap the strings with the right-hand index finger at the appropriate fret to produce a harmonic with a percussive sound.

harmonics   The notes of the harmonic series that sound clear and bell-like when played, produced by lightly touching a string at various points on the fretboard and indicated in notation with diamond-shaped symbols.

harmony   The result of two or more tones played simultaneously.

head   A slang term for the A section or primary theme of a song. This section tends to introduce the theme and is played true to the melody with no alteration or improvisation.

hinge barre   The technique of hinging an extended finger either from its tip or its base to allow a barre chord to be placed more easily.

interval   The distance in pitch between notes.

isolation   To continually repeat a difficult movement form slowly and accurately to reinforce positive habits when performing a section of music.

key   The tonal center of a piece of music.

key signature   The group of sharps or flats that appears at the beginning of a piece of music to indicate what key the music is in.

ledger lines   Short horizontal lines used to extend a staff either higher or lower.

legato   To play notes smoothly and without separate attacks.

lute   A fretted, plucked instrument with 7 to 14 courses popular in Europe during the 15th and 16th centuries.

major chord   A chord consisting of a root, a major third, and a perfect fifth.

major scale   The most common scale in music, consisting of a specific order of whole and half steps: W–W–H–W–W–W–H.

major third   A note that is four half steps up from the root.

measure (or bar)   Divisions of the staff that are separated by bar lines and contain equal numbers of beats.

menuett   German form of *minuet.*

midrange position   An area in the hand's range of motion midway between total flexion and total extension. This position provides maximum leverage and allows the hands to work most efficiently.

minor chord   A chord consisting of a root, a minor third, and a perfect fifth.

minor third   A note that is three half steps up from the root.

minuet   A country dance, usually in $\frac{3}{4}$ time, that originated in France around 1650.

modality   The different musical colors created by using various scales and modes, generally described as major or minor.

mode   A set of notes arranged into a specific pattern of whole steps and half steps, derived from either the major or minor scale.

monophonic   A single line in music having no accompaniment or harmony played along with it.

mordent (upper, lower, sharped)   A rapid alternation between the written note and its upper or lower neighboring tone in the key. If sharp, raise the note one half step from its tone in the key.

motif   The main theme or musical figure in a piece of music. It tends to be repeated or developed throughout a piece.

movement form   Any movement on the guitar, from one chord to the next or one note to the next. Even the simple action of sounding a string can be called a movement form.

mute   To stop a note from ringing on the guitar by placing either the right or left hand over the strings.

natural   A symbol that indicates a note is not sharp or flat.

note   A symbol used to represent a musical tone.

nut   The part of the guitar at the top of the neck that aligns the strings over the fretboard.

octave   The interval between two immediate notes of the same name, equivalent to 12 frets on the guitar, or eight scale steps.

open position   Fingering for chords that incorporates open strings and no barre.

opus   Meaning "work," a numbering system used to chronologize a composer's works.

ornament, ornamentation   Various techniques used to embellish a melodic line with additional notes, rhythms, or harmonies. Mordents, trills, turns, and appoggiaturas are all ornaments.

ostinato   A musical figure or motif that continuously repeats.

palm mute   A technique of muffling the guitar strings with the right hand palm at the bridge of the guitar.

parallel major, parallel minor   A major and minor scale that share the same tonic, such as E major and E minor.

pavane   A slow, procession-like 16th-century Italian dance form.

pedal   A sustained tone, usually in the bass.

pick   A device used to pluck or strum the strings of a guitar.

pima   Abbreviations for the right-hand fingers in fingerpicking notation: p = thumb, i = index finger, m = middle finger, and a = ring finger.

pitch   The location of a note related to its lowness or highness.

pizzicato   A choppy muted sound produced by muting the bridge with a palm mute.

plectrum   A pick used to play the guitar.

polyphony   The relationship between multiple voices. Textures created by two or more independent musical voices.

position   The location of the hand on the fretboard at a particular fret, as determined by the position of the 1st finger. For example, if the 1st finger is over the 5th fret, the hand is in 5th position.

power chord   A chord consisting of only the root and fifth, with no third or additional notes. When played as barre chords on an electric guitar with distortion, power chords can create a wall of sound.

preludio   Typically the introductory movement of a baroque suite, often designed to warm up the fingers.

pull-off   A left hand technique in which two notes are fingered on the same string, and the lower note is then made to sound by pulling the fretting finger off the higher note.

quarter note   A note equal to one beat in $\frac{4}{4}$ time and the basic unit of musical time.

quarter rest   A rest equal to the duration of a quarter note.

rasgueado   A right-hand flamenco technique in which the fingers extend rapidly to brush across the strings in a percussive fashion. A powerful form of strumming used to punctuate a musical line.

recapitulation   The return of the main theme, to reprise.

relative major or minor   Scales that are relative share the same key signature. For example, C major's relative minor is A minor. A minor's relative major is C major.

Renaissance period   Music historians have given this title to the time period approximately between 1500 and 1600. See Appendix D.

repeat signs   A group of various symbols indicating sections of music to be played over again.

rest   A symbol representing measured silence in music.

rest stroke   A right-hand finger stroke that allows the finger to rest on an adjacent string after sounding a note.

rhythm   The musical organization of beats.

riff   A short, repeated melodic pattern.

romanesca   A musical form that has at its foundation four chords that continuously repeat for the purpose of improvisation. A Spanish form whose earliest example can be found in Narváez's "Guardame las Vacas."

romantic period   Music historians have given this title to the time period approximately between 1820 and 1910. See Appendix D.

root note   The fundamental note of a chord, and also the note that gives the chord its letter name. The root is the first note of the corresponding major scale.

rubato   To "rob" time; to slightly adjust the rhythmic grouping of a phrase to imply direction and emotion. A slight speeding up and slowing down that reflects the mood of the music. To play without rubato would make the performance sterile and machine-like or metronomic.

saltarello   A lively dance form dating back to the 13th century.

sarabande   A slow and stately 17th-century dance form, usually used for the third movement of a baroque suite, generally in triple meter with the accent on the second beat.

scale   A set of notes arranged in a specific order of whole steps and half steps. The most common scale is the major scale.

sextuplet   A sequence of six notes played in the time of four, dividing the beat into a number of equal subdivisions. Emphasizing *p* and *a* will create a duple feeling of two subdivisions, and emphasizing *p* and *m* will result in a triple feeling of three subdivisions.

sharp   A symbol that indicates to raise a note one half step.

sixteenth note   A note equal to half an eighth note, or one quarter of a beat in $\frac{4}{4}$ time.

sixteenth rest   A rest equal to the duration of a sixteenth note.

slide   A technique of moving smoothly from one note to another. A note is fingered by the left hand and played by the right hand, then the left hand finger maintains pressure while sliding quickly on the string to the next note without interrupting the sound or picking the note again. Indicated in notation with a diagonal line between notes.

sonorous   The quality of a sound having depth or resonant character. A guitar is more sonorous than a lute, for example.

staccato   To play notes in a short, detached manner. Indicated in notation by a dot directly over or under the note or chord.

staff   The horizontal lines and spaces upon which music notes are placed to designate their pitch.

standard tuning   The normal tuning for the guitar in which the strings are tuned from low to high E–A–D–G–B–E.

sul ponticello   To play with the right hand close to the bridge of the guitar to create a bright and brittle sound.

sul tasto   To play with the right hand close to the fretboard for a dark and mellow sound.

suspension   A situation in which a nonchord tone is played with the chord to create dissonance that then resolves downward to consonance. The addition of a perfect 4th to a major triad will create a suspension that would then resolve to the 3rd. The same can be done with a major 6th resolving to the 5th or major 2nd resolving to the tonic.

sympathetic motion   The movement of the fingers as they flex and extend together as a group when playing notes and chords. The fingers are said to *move in sympathy* or to *move sympathetically*.

syncopation   A shift of rhythmic emphasis to the weak beat, or to a weak part of a beat.

TAB   Abbreviation for *tablature*.

tablature   A system of guitar notation that uses a graphic representation of the six strings of the guitar with numbers indicating which fret to play. There have been many tablature systems over the ages and many of them are associated with various nationalities. The French, Italians, Germans, and Spanish all had different systems, some using numbers, some letters, and others even reversing the order of the strings. The Renaissance system that most closely represents what is used today would have been Luys Milán's system, first published in 1536.

tempo   The speed at which music is played.

theme and variation   A musical form in which a theme is introduced and followed by a series of variations.

theorbo   A large, 12-coursed lute.

thumb sweep   The technique of sweeping across the strings with the right-hand thumb.

tie   A curved line that joins two or more notes of the same pitch, indicating to play them as one continuous note.

time signature   A sign resembling a fraction that appears at the beginning of a piece of music. The top number indicates how many beats are in each measure and the bottom number indicates what kind of note gets one beat.

tip joint   The first joint from the end of your finger. On the right hand this joint should be firm enough to develop a good sound, but not so firm that it catches or hooks on a string and not so loose that it collapses.

tonic   The first note in a scale. C is the tonic of a C scale.

treatise   A book, such as a method book, that teaches a particular subject.

treble clef   A symbol at the beginning of the staff that designates the second line as the note G. Also called the *G clef.*

tremolo   Rapid repetition of a single note performed by the right hand.

trill   Rapid alternation between a written note and its neighboring note, either above or below.

triplet   A group of three notes played in the time of two.

unison   The same pitch played at the same time on different strings of the guitar.

up-pick   To pick the string upward, toward the ceiling.

up-stroke   To strike the strings upward, toward the ceiling.

up-strum   To strum the strings upward, toward the ceiling.

vihuela   A six-coursed, fretted, plucked guitar-shaped instrument played in Spain during the 15th and 16th centuries. Tuned like the top six courses of a lute, it is also known as the *vihuela de mano.*

viol   A bowed instrument common in the 16th and 17th centuries that was a precursor to the violin.

viola da gamba   A viol held on or between the legs, similar to the modern cello.

whole note   A note equal to four quarter notes, or four beats in $\frac{4}{4}$ time.

whole rest   A rest equal to the duration of a whole note, or the duration of any full measure.

whole step   The distance of two half steps, or two frets on the guitar.

wrist joint   Three joints allow for the movement of the thumb—the tip joint is closest to the nail of the thumb, the middle joint comes next and is where most people tend to move their thumb from, and finally there's the wrist joint which is actually found back at the wrist. This is actually where we want to move our thumb from when sounding a bass string with the right hand. The tendency for the other joints to move should be minimized.

MCAT®

Psychology and Sociology Review

2nd Edition

The Staff of The Princeton Review

The Princeton Review®

The Princeton Review
24 Prime Parkway, Suite 201
Natick, MA 01760
E-mail: editorialsupport@review.com

Published in the United States by Penguin Random House LLC, New York, and in Canada by Random House of Canada, a division of Penguin Random House Ltd., Toronto.

The Princeton Review is not affiliated with Princeton University.

MCAT is a registered trademark of the Association of American Medical Colleges, which is not affiliated with The Princeton Review.

ISBN: 978-1-101-92060-2
ISSN: 2332-8495

Editor: Sarah Litt
Production Artist: Craig Patches
Production Editor: Beth Hanson

Printed in the United States of America on partially recycled paper.

10 9 8 7 6

2nd edition

Editorial

Rob Franek, Senior VP, Publisher
Casey Cornelius, VP Content Development
Mary Beth Garrick, Director of Production
Selena Coppock, Managing Editor
Meave Shelton, Senior Editor
Colleen Day, Editor
Sarah Litt, Editor
Aaron Riccio, Editor
Orion McBean, Editorial Assistant

Random House Publishing Team

Tom Russell, Publisher
Alison Stoltzfus, Publishing Manager
Melinda Ackell, Associate Managing Editor
Ellen Reed, Production Manager
Kristin Lindner, Production Supervisor
Andrea Lau, Designer